The Jewish Presence
in
Early British Records, 1650 - 1850

Compiled by
David Dobson

CLEARFIELD

Printed for Clearfield Company by
Genealogical Publishing Company
Baltimore, Maryland
2014

ISBN 978-0-8063-5688-4

INTRODUCTION

There had been a Jewish presence in England since the days of William the Conqueror however in 1290 King Edward I of England banished them from his possessions. From that date until 1655 when Oliver Cromwell encouraged them to return there were officially no Jews in England. In Scotland there had been no similar legislation banning Jews though few, if any, settled there in the medieval period. During the seventeenth century the activities of the Spanish Inquisition encouraged Sephardic Jews to emigrate, some went north to the Netherlands while other moved to Brazil. Oliver Cromwell, recognizing the skills of these Jews, persuaded some of them to move to London and later to English American colonies such as Barbados and Jamaica. In due course some of their descendants settled in the American colonies. A colony of Marrano merchants was established in London which carried out substantial trade from there to the Netherlands, Iberia, Brazil, the East and West Indies. Later there was an influx of Jews from Germany, Poland and Russia which became significant in the late nineteenth century. These Ashkenazi Jews arrived and initially settled in east coast ports from Dundee south to London, later many moved to industrial cities such as Glasgow, Leeds, and Liverpool, and some moved abroad to North America, South Africa and Australasia.

This source book attempts to identify some of the Jews in British records from the mid seventeenth century to the mid nineteenth century. In some of the records of the seventeenth century there are specific references to people identified as being Jewish, later Hebrew forenames coupled with surnames sometimes in conjunction with occupation or place of birth were used to identify people of Jewish origin. Much care has been in selecting entries as this latter method has drawbacks in that many Gentiles use Biblical names.

David Dobson

Dundee, Scotland, 2014.

AARON, DAVID, a German Jew, was granted a pass to travel from England to Holland, 25 September 1706. [TNA.SP44.393.100]

AARONS, HENRY, born 1801 son of **Solomon Aarons**, a stationer in Liverpool in 1841, died 1874. [Deane Road Cemetery, Liverpool] [Census]

AARON, JONATHAN, a poor Jew, was granted a pass to travel from England to Holland, 10 October 1706. [TNA.SP44.393.172]

AARON, MOSES, in Ludford, Herefordshire, probate 1658 PCC. [TNA]

ABARBANEL, DAVID, a petitioner in London, 1658. [SPDom.Commonwealth.cxxv.58]

ABARBANEL, PHINEAS, an alien, was granted denization, 3 June 1699. [Patent Roll, 11 William III, part 2.]

ABENDANA, JACOB, born 1630 in Spain, son of **Joseph Abendana,** Hakham of the Spanish and Portuguese Synagogues in London from 1680, died 12 September 1695. [TJS.iii.43]

ABENDANA, ISAAC, a scholar, who arrived in England with his brother **Jacob Abendana,** 16..., a Hebrew teacher in Oxford. [TJS.iii.43]

ABENDANA, RAPHAEL, an alien, was granted denization, 9 March 1694. [Patent Roll, 6 William and Mary, part 1][S.P.Dom. Warrant book 38.496]; in Boston, New England, 1696. [TNA.HCA. 61.Lopez,versus,Anthony];on Nevis 1708, [TNA.CO.152-157]; resettled on Nevis, 1712. [JTP.1709-1715.386]

ABOF, ISACK, in St Michael's parish, Barbados, 1679. [TNA.CO1.44.47]; with 2 children {?} in St Michael's 1680. [TNA.CO1]

ABRAHAM, AGNUS, from Barbados aboard the ketch <u>Francis and Susan</u> bound for Boston, New England, 1679. [TNA.CO1]

ABRAHAMS, ALEXANDER, born 1751, a clerk from London, an indentured servant aboard the <u>London Packet</u> bound for Philadelphia in 1774. [TNA.T47.9/11]

ABRAHAM, ALFRED, a decree, 24 May 1848. [NAS.SC39.17.11133]

ABRAHAM, HAYEM, bound from Barbados aboard the ship <u>James</u> for New York, 1678. [TNA.CO1]

ABRAHAM, ISAAC, grant of denization, 16 December 1687. [S.P.Dom.Car II, Entry book 67]

ABRAHAM, BAR., a German Jew, was granted a pass to travel from England to Holland, 6 August 1706. [TNA.SP44.393.51]

ABRAHAM, Mrs ELIZABETH, in Antigua, a deposition, 1718. [JTP. 1718.361]

ABRAHAM, HESEKIA, a poor Jew, was granted a pass to travel from England to Holland, 23 October 1706. [TNA.SP44.393.179]

ABRAHAM, ISAAC, a German Jew, was granted a pass to travel from England to Holland, 30 April 1706. [TNA.SP44.390.443]

ABRAHAM, ISRAEL, an articifer in Ipswich, Suffolk, 1796. [TJS.ii.134]; died 12 February 5602 aged 86. [Jewish Cemetery, St Clement's, Ipswich]

ABRAHAM, JACOB, an optician and mathematical instrument maker, Bartlett Street, Bath, 1800.

ABRAHAM, LEA, in Duke's Place, parish of St James, London, 1695. [LRS.1966.1]

ABRAHAM, MICHAEL, born 1781, died 7 September 1859. [Betholom MI, Birmingham]; aged 58, a fruiterer, **Hyam** aged 18, **Bloema**{?}aged 54, **Sarah** aged 27, **Catharine** aged 24, **Phoebe** aged 21, Persho St., Birmingham, 1841. [Census]

ABRAHAM, MORDECAI, with his wife **Rebecca** and daughter **Rachel,** in Duke's Place, parish of St James, London, 1695. [LRS.1966.1]

ABRAHAM, PHILLIP, in Antigua, a deposition, 1718. [JTP.1718.361]

ABRAHAM, RAPHAEL, a German Jew, was granted a pass to travel from England to Holland, 30 April 1706. [TNA.SP44.390.443]

ABRAHAM, SALOMAN, a German Jew, was granted a pass to travel from England to Holland, 16 August 1706. [TNA.SP44.393.61]

ABRAINZI, ABRAM, took the Oath of Association in New York, 1696. [TNA]

ABRAMS, ISAACH, took the Oath of Association in New York, 1696. [TNA]

ABUDIENTE, ABRAHAM, from Barbados aboard the ketch <u>Phoenix</u> bound for Antigua in November 1679. [TNA.CO1]

ABUDIENTE, ROWLAND, a merchant in London, freeman of London, 1697

ADOLPH, JACOB, an alien, was granted denization, 13 May 1700. [Patent Roll, 12 William III, part 4]

ADOLPHUS, JACOB, graduated MD from King's College, Aberdeen, 1816. [KCA]

ADAMITE, BEERSHEBA, a servant in the parish of St Dionis Backchurch, London, 1695. [LRS.1966.1]

ADLER, NATHAN MARCUS, born in Hanover on 13 January 1803, Orthodox Chief Rabbi of the British Empire from 1845, died 21 January 1890.

AGUILAR, ABRAHAM, in London, son of **Emanuel Aguilar** in Jamaica, a deed re plantations in Jamaica, 1784. [Car.2.330]

AGUILAR, ISAAC, a merchant, formerly in Jamaica, later of Devonshire Square, London, an indenture, 1802. [Car.2.367]

AGUILAR, JOSEPH, in London, son of **Emanuel Aguilar** in Jamaica, a deed re plantations in Jamaica, 1784. [Car.2.330]

AGUILAR, JOSEPH, and his wife **Grace**, of Devonshire Square, Bishopsgate Street, London, an indenture, 6 November 1802. [Car. 2.367]

AGUILAR, JUDITH, a widow in Devonshire Square, London, an indenture, 1814. [Car.2.369]

AGILLIER, RAPHAELL, born in Spain, a widow, grant of denization, 27 June 1627. [Patent Roll, 3 Charles I, part 13]

AHRENS, STATZ, born in Lunenburg, Saxony, son of **John Ahrens,** a grant of naturalization, 1670. [Patent Roll, 22 Car ii.37]

AIS, REITZA, born in Wilna, Russia, 1824, died 4 July 1880. [Newington MI, Edinburgh]

ALEXANDER, LEVI, an articifer in Colchester, Essex, 1796. [TJS.ii.134]; died 10 February 5571 aged 63. [Jewish Cemetery, St Clement's, Ipswich, Suffolk]

ALEXANDER, SALOMON, a German Jew, was granted a pass to travel from England to Holland, 3 January 1706. [TNA.SP44.390.363]

ALION, SOLOMON, with his wife **Oro** and daughters **Grace** and **Hester,** in the parish of St Katherine, Coleman, London, 1695. [LRS.1955.4]

ALMAN, AARON, a silversmith in Bristol, 1793. [Bristol Directory, 1793/1794]

ALMAN, ISAAC, a watchmaker in Bristol, 1793. [Bristol Directory, 1793/1794]

ALVARANGUES, SAMUEL, and his wife **Rebecca,** in the parish of Allhallows, London Wall, 1695. [LRS.1966.5]

ALVAREZE, ARON, in the parish of All Hallows, London Wall, 1695. [LRS.1966.5]

ALVARES, DUARTE HENRIQUES, a petitioner in London, 1658. [SPDom.Commonwealth.cxxv.58]

ALVARES, SAMUEL, an alien, born in Bayonne, France, was granted denization, 1 September 1669. [Patent Roll, 21 Charles II, part 2]

ALVARINGO, DAVID, with his wife **Abigail,** in the parish of St James, Duke's Place, London, 1695. [LRS.1966.5]

ALVERENGA, JOSEPH DA COSTA, born in Portugal, a grant of denization, in June 1670. [Patent Roll, 22 Car ii]

ALVERUS, DAVID, wife **Sarah,** and daughters **Zipporah, Miriam,** and **Grace,** in the parish of St Andrew Undershaft, London, 1695. [LRS. 1966.5]

AMADEUS, ALEXANDER, from Florence, Italy, was appointed to the Chair of Hebrew at Edinburgh University in 1679. [OSJ.1/6]

AMOS, ARON, and his wife **Hester,** in the parish of St Augustine, London, 1695. [LRS.1966.5]

AMES, LEVI, a merchant in Bristol trading with South Carolina, 1773. [TNA.E190.1229.4]; lease of Queen Square, Bristol, 1789. [BRO.814.1D]

ANDRADE, ABRAHAM, born 1750, a clerk and book-keeper, bound from London aboard the Minerva for Philadelphia, 1774. [TNA.T47.9/11]

ANSELL, ANSELL, an articifer in Ipswich, Suffolk, 1796. [TJS.ii.134]

ANTONIUS, GABRIEL, a Jew in Surinam petitioned to go to Jamaica, 1676. [SPAWI.1676.818.i]; in St Michael's parish, Barbados, 1679. [TNA.CO1.44.47]; with 2 children {?} in St Michael's 1680. [TNA.CO1]

APPLE, HARRIS, born in Prussia during 1811, a traveller in Quarrington, Lincoln, 1841. [Census]; a tailor, draper and hatter, 42 Lowgate, Hull, Yorkshire, 1852. [HCA]

ARABUS, MOSES, a militiaman in Barbados, 1680. [TNA.CO1.44.47]

ARIES, DIEGO RODRIGUES, a petitioner in London, 1658. [SPDom.Commonwealth.cxxv.58]

ARIOS, ISAAC, with his wife **Abigail,** son **Abraham** and daughter **Hester,** in Allhallows, London Wall, 1695. [LRS.1966.8]

ARON, ABRAHAM BURGOS, in St Michael's parish, Barbados, 1679. [TNA.CO1.44.47]; with 2 children {?} in St Michael's 1680. [TNA.CO1]

ARONS, JOSEPH, from Amsterdam, Holland, landed at Gravesend, Kent, settled in Edinburgh by 1803. [EBR:SL115][FJC.5]

ARONS, SHONTE, from Amsterdam, Holland, landed at Gravesend, Kent, settled in Edinburgh by 1803. [EBR:SL115][FJC.5]

ARROBAS, HANANIAH, resettled on Nevis, 1712. [JTP.1709-1715.386]

ARROBAS, MOSES, a militiaman in St Michael's parish, Barbados, 1679. [TNA.CO1.44.47]; with 4 children {?} in St Michael's 1680. [TNA.CO1]

ARRALONA, SAMUEL, in the parish of St Helen, London, 1695.[LRS. 1966.9]

ASABEE, DAVID, a militiaman in Barbados, 1679. [TNA.CO1.44.47]

ASHENHEIM, JACOB B., a merchant in Edinburgh, 1825, [FJC.6]; burgess of Edinburgh in 1828, [EBR]; a burgess of Glasgow, 1829, [GBR]; jeweller in Edinburgh, trustee of **Philip Levy,** 1829. [NRS.CS44.174.64]; **ASHENHEIM, J.,** a jeweller and watchmaker, 61 North Bridge Street, Edinburgh, 1835, a jeweller at 103 Princes Street, Edinburgh, 1849. [EPOD]; a jeweller, 4 Leopold Place, Edinburgh, died 28 December 1860, inventory 1861, Commissariat of Edinburgh. [NRS]; husband of **Malky Aaron** 1813, parents of **Lewis, Charles, Jane** and **Hannah.**

ASHENHEIM, CHARLES, born in Edinburgh, son of **Jacob Ashenheim** and his wife **Malky Aaron,** emigrated to New South Wales, Australia. [FJC.34]

ASHENHEIM, ESTHER TOBY, born 1834 in Poland, wife of Isaac Ashenheim, died 14 December 1896. [Newington MI, Edinburgh] [Census]

ASHENHEIM, ISAAC, born 1820, died in January 1879. [Newington MI, Edinburgh]

ASHENHEIM, LEWIS, born in Edinburgh 1816, a medical student at Edinburgh University, 1836, graduated MD from St Andrews in 1839, later a physician in Jamaica, died there on 22 October 1858, buried in the Jewish cemetery at Falmouth, Jamaica. [SCHR.III.204][OSJ.14/15] [BRSA.33]

ASHENHEIM, MATILDA, born about 1796 in 'foreign parts', a jeweller, 22 George Street, Edinburgh, 1841. [Census]

ASHENHEIM, MICHAEL, died 20 January AM5612 'in the prime of life'. [JBGE]

ASHER, ASHER, born in Glasgow 16 February 1837, educated at Glasgow High School and at Glasgow University, a physician in Bishopbriggs and after 1862 in London, died in London on 7 January 1889. [SCJ.25][1841 Census]

ASHER, LEVI, a felon, transported from London aboard the Tayloe bound for Virginia in July 1773. [TNA.T53]

ASHER, PHILLIP, born 1806 'in foreign parts' [Lublin, Poland], 5 King Street, Glasgow, wife **Hannah,** born 1816, 'in foreign parts', son **Asher,** born 1836 in Glasgow, son **William** born 1838 in Glasgow, and daughter **Rebecca** born 1840 in Glasgow. [Census] [SCJ.25]

ASCHERSON, DEBORAH, was buried outside the Necropolis walls in Glasgow, August 1847. [SCJ.23]

ASSER, NATHAN, wife **Sarah,** and son **Nathan,** and daughter **Sarah,** in the parish of St Faith under St Paul's, London, 1695, [LRS.1966.9]

ATHIAS, MOSES ISRAEL, in London 16... [TJS.i.69]

ATKINS, SARAH, in St Michael's parish, Barbados, 1679. [TNA.CO1.44.47]; with 1 child{?} in St Michael's 1680. [TNA.CO1]

AUERBACH, EZEKIAL CASPAR, born 1795, a hawker from Warsaw, in Inverness, 1830. [CJ.7]

AVIERS, ABRAHAM, with his wife, in the parish of St Katharine Cree, London, 1695. [LRS.1966.43]

AVIERS, JACOB, with his wife, sons **Aaron** and **Moses,** and daughter **Sarah,** in the parish of St Katharine Cree, London, 1695. [LRS.1966.11]

AVILA, SAMUEL, a bachelor, with brother **David** a bachelor, sister **Rachel** and **Hannah,** in the parish of St Katharine, Coleman, London, 1695. [LRS.1966.11]

AVIONS, SCHONTIE, aged 40, born in Amsterdam, residing in Canongate, Edinburgh, by 1803. [EBR.SL115]

AVIONS, TOSERS, aged 40, born in Amsterdam, an umbrella maker in Canongate, Edinburgh, by 1803. [EBR.SL115]

BALISSA, JOHN SOLOMON, born 1743, a footman from London, emigrated from London aboard the Russia Merchant bound for Maryland in 1774. [TNA.T47.9/11]

BALLIN, Dr DE., born 1771 'in foreign parts', physician and a teacher of German, Thorter Row, Dundee, 1837. [DD][Census]

BALLIN, ISAAC SAMUEL, born 1811 in Wells, Somerset, a fur manufacturer at 26 High Street, Bristol, 1832, residing in Barton Street, Bristol, 1841; married [1] **Susanna Ballin**, daughter of **Samuel Ballin** and his wife **Elizabeth Whittern** in Bristol on 25 September 1833 [she died in 1849]; parents of **Fanny** born 1834, **Maria** born 1837, and **Emma** born 1840; from 1836 to 1855 he was a fur manufacturer and importer in Bristol, in 1858 he moved to London where he was a furrier and straw hat dealer until his death there 1 December 1897, he married [2] **Annie Moss.** [1841 Census]

BARICTSGOK, AUVOHOM, a German Jew, was granted a pass to travel from England to Holland, 11 April 1706. [TNA.SP44.390.423]

BARNED, ISRAEL, born 1777 in Portsmouth, a watchmaker and jeweller in Liverpool, died 1858. [Deane Road Cemetery, Liverpool]

BARNETT, ABRAHAM, born 1811 in Poland, residing in Hull, wife **Hannah** born 1813 in Hull, son **Barnard** born 1840 in Hull, son **Jacob** born 1850 in Hull, daughter **Julia** born 1843 in Hull, and daughter **Rosetta** born 1847 in Hull. [Census]; cloth dealer, 113 High dealer, Hull, Yorkshire, 1843. [HCA]

BARNETT, ABRAHAM, born Manchester 1818, a hawker, 46 St Leonard Street, Edinburgh, died 29 June 1851, aged 34, erected by his brother **John Barnett** in 1859; **Caroline Barnett**? 18..., aged 26?; **Jessie Barnett,** wife of ...Davis. [JBGE][Braid MI, Edinburgh][Census]

BARNETT, ISAAC, aged 19, a weaver from Stepney, London, son of **Martha Barnett**, an indentured servant bound from London to Maryland in 1725. [CLRO]

BARNET, JACOB, from Italy, a secretary at Oxford 1610-1612, later adviser on Jewish matters at the French Court.

BARNETT, Reverend RAPHAEL, born in Poland 1814, died in Liverpool 1887. [Deane Road Cemetery, Liverpool]

BARNETT, ZIPPARAH, wife of **Isaac Barnett,** died 17 March 1857. [Betholom MI, Birmingham]

BARONS, GEORGE, born in Bockhorne, Oldenburg, son of Bernard Barons, a grant of naturalisation, 1670. [Patent Roll, 22 Car ii.37]

BARON, SAMUEL, 'born beyond the seas', a merchant, a grant of denization, 31 August 1671. [Patent Roll, 23 Car ii.6]

BARREW, ABRAHAM, a merchant, with his wife **Rebecca,** daughter **Luna,** and son **Aaron,** in the parish of St James, Duke's Place, London, 1695. [LRS.1966.19]

BARREW, MOSES, with his wife **Rachel,** son **Mordecai,** and daughter **Sarah,** in the parish of St James, Duke's Place, London, 1695. [LRS. 1966.19]; an alien, was granted denization, 4 November 1699. [Patent Roll, 11 William III, pt.3.]

BARRUCH, ABRAHAM, a cavalryman in St Michael's parish, Barbados, 1679. [TNA.CO1.44.47]; with 3 children {?} in St Michael's 1680. [TNA.CO1]

BARRUCH, AARON, a cavalryman in St Michael's parish, Barbados, 1679. [TNA.CO1.44.47]; with 5 children {?} in St Michael's 1680. [TNA.CO1]

BARUCH, DANIEL, a Member of the Royal College of Surgeons, proposed by Drs J. Sequira and J. H. Myers in London, graduated MD from King's College, Aberdeen, 1816. [KCA.154]

BARRUCH, REBECCA, in St Michael's parish, Barbados, 1679. [TNA.CO1.44.47]; with 1 child{?} in St Michael's 1680. [TNA.CO1]

BARSILEY, JOSEPH, and his wife **Ester,** German Jews, were granted a pass to travel from England to Holland, 10 January 1706. [TNA.SP44.390.365]

BARUH, DANIEL, MRCS, graduated MD from King's College, Aberdeen, on 12 September 1816, recommended by Drs J. Sequiera and J. H. Myers in London. [KCA]

BARUH, ISAAC, of London, a deed re plantations in Jamaica, 1784. [Car.2.330]

BARUK, MOSES, a Jew in Surinam petitioned to go to Jamaica, 1676. [SPAWI.1676.818.i]

BASAN, SAMUEL, a German Jew, was granted a pass to travel from England to Holland, 24 June 1706. [TNA.SP44.393.14]

BEHRANS, ELIZABETH, grocer, 47 King Street, Dundee, Angus, 1829; 66/68 King Street, Dundee, 1840. [DD]; born 1801 in Monifieth, Angus, a linen draper, 6 Bain Square, Dundee, 1851, son **John Behrens,** born 1826 in Dundee, a linen merchant's clerk, daughter **Marion Behrens,** born 1833 in Dundee, assistant in linen draper's shop. [Census]

BEHREND, DAVID, born 1792 in Hanover, a ship-broker in Liverpool, died 1863. [Deane Road Cemetery, Liverpool]

BEHREND, GEORGE, born 1826, a merchant and ship-owner in Liverpool. [LRO.296beh]

BEHRENS, ..., a ship-owner in London, 1712. [TNA.HCA.Vol. 84.Exams]

BELZARO, ISAACK MENDEZ, his wife **Rachel,** sons **Abraham, Isaack, Aaron, David,** and daughters **Judith, Hester, Leer,** and **Rebecca,** in the parish of St James, Duke's Place, London, 1695. [LRS.1966.25]

BENAS, LOUIS, born 1820 in Prussia, a banker in Liverpool, died 1890. [Deane Road Cemetery, Liverpool]

BENGER, ISAAC, in the parish of All Hallows, Barking, London, 1695. [LRS.1966.25]

BEN ISRAEL, MENASSEH, a petitioner in London, 1658. [SPDom.Commonwealth.cxxv.58][SPDom.1655/56.118, 128,14, 58]

BENJAMIN, BENJAMIN S., aged 32, born in Hamburg, a merchant in Edinburgh by 1818. [EBR.SL115]

BENJAMIN, ISRAEL, visited Hull, Yorkshire, in 1734. [Holy Trinity Church records, Hull]

BENMAN, ZOPHER, in the parish of St Dunstan in the East, London, 1695. [LRS.1966.25]

BENNETT, ISAAC, with wife **Sarah,** son **Isaac,** and daughter **Hannah,** in the parish of St Dionis Backchurch, London, 1695. [LRS.1966.25]

BENSON, REUBEN, 1793. [NRS.CS235.B18.12]

BER JOSAFAT, J. ISRAEL, [alias Paul Julius Reuter], born 1816 in Prussia, a grant of naturalization, 17 March 1857, died 1899. [TNA.HO. 1.79.2403]

BEREND, M., a teacher aged 34, born in Altona, Saxony, settled in Edinburgh by 1813. [EBR.SL115]

BERLIN, or BEVILLEN, FRANCIS, alias **ABRAHAM BURNET or BARNET,** drawing master, Leith Walk, Edinburgh, process of divorce, 1790. [NRS.CC8.6.853]

BERLU, JACOB JOHN, born in Franckford, Germany, son of **John Moe Berlu,** a grant of naturalisation, 1670. [Patent Office, 22 Car ii.37]

BERNAL, ABRAHAM, probate 1790 PCC. [TNA]

BERNAL, ISAAC, junior, merchant in Crutched Friars, London, a contract, 1776. [Car.3.157]

BERNAL, JACOB ISRAEL, in Kingston, Jamaica, an indenture, 1782, witnessed by **Thomas Myers Bernal** in Queen Square, Holburn, London, a letter 1787. [Car.3.158]; late of Kingston, Jamaica, later in London, an indenture, 1798. [Car.3.25]

??BERNERS, JANE, born 1745, a cook and maid from London, an indentured servant aboard the Adventurer bound from London to Virginia in 1775. [TNA.T47.9/11]

BEWICK, RUBEN, a German Jew, was granted a pass to travel from England to Holland, 23 September 1706. [TNA.SP44.393.95]

BLANK, HEZEKIAH, an indentured servant bound from Bristol to Virginia in 1677. [BRO]

BLANKENSEE, JULIA, wife of **Solomon Blankensee,** died 15 December 1858. [Betholom MI, Birmingham]

BLOCH, ELIAS, born 1838, died 12 February 1896. [Dundee MI]

BLOOMGARDEN, RUSHE, born 1825, died 11 October 1903. [Piershill MI, Edinburgh]

BOABE, ABRAHAM, a German Jew, was granted a pass to travel from England to Holland, 22 April 1706. [TNA.SP44.390.436]

BOYNA, DANIEL, a cavalryman in St Michael's parish, Barbados, 1679. [TNA.CO1.44.47]; with 3 children {?} in St Michael's 1680. [TNA.CO1]

BRILL, ESTER, a servant in the parish of St John the Baptist, London, 1695. [LRS.1966.41]

BRAHAM, JAMES, alias **Zachariah Abrahams,** born 1811 in Plymouth, son of **David Abrahams** [1763-1840] and his wife **Rose Jacobs** [1776-1842], a goldsmith and clockmaker, died 5 February 1873. [Deane Road Cemetery, Liverpool]

BRANDON, ABIGAIL, widow administratrix of **Isaac Pereira Brandon,** a petitioner in Jamaica, 1752. [ActsPCCol.1745-1766.151]

BRATH, ISRAEL, from Poland, a dealer in Hull, Yorkshire, 1797. [HCA.C.BRE.7.1.54]

BRIGHT, HENRY, a merchant in Bristol trading with Philadelphia, 1773. [TNA.E190.1229.4]

BRIGHT, ISAAC, born circa 1762, a jeweller and silversmith, died 1849, husband of **Ann Micholls** born circa 1775, died 1847, parents of **Maurice** [1798-1849], **Selim** [1799-1811], **Henry** [born 1817], **Rebecca** [1814-1838], and others. [Deane Road Cemetery, Liverpool]

BRODUM, WILLIAM, graduated MD in Aberdeen, 1791 [CJ]

BROWN, DAVID, a merchant in Edinburgh, 1691. [EBR]

BROWN, REBECCA, born 1842, died 24 April 1907. [Newington MI, Edinburgh]

BUCINO, DANIEL, a merchant in Barbados, a petition, 1681. [SPAWI. 1681.198]

BUENO, BENJAMIN, in Christchurch parish, Barbados, 1679. [TNA.CO1.44.47]

BUENO, DANIEL, a cavalryman in St Michael's parish, Barbados, 1682. [ActsPCCol.1682.423]

BUENO, JOSEPH, an alien, granted denization, 2 October 1662. [Patent Roll, 14 Car. Ii.2]

BUENO, JOSEPH, took the Oath of Association in New York, 1696. [TNA]

BURGOS, ABRAHAM, from Barbados aboard the ketch William and John bound to New England in 1679 [TNA.CO1]

BURGOS, ELIAS, a militiaman in Barbados, 1679. [TNA.CO1.44.47]

BURGOS, IRMIAHU or JEREMIAH, an alien, a grant of denization, 10 December 1695. [Patent Roll, 7 Wm. iii, part 4]

BURGIS, JEREMIAH, a militiaman in Barbados, 1679. [TNA.CO1.44.47]

BURGIS, MOSES, a militiaman in Barbados, 1679. [TNA.CO1.44.47]

BURGOS, RACHEL, in St Michael's parish, Barbados, 1679. [TNA.CO1.44.47]; with 6 children {?} in St Michael's 1680. [TNA.CO1]

BUSVINE, JOHN, in Bristol, 1840. [BRO.5074.3]

CALIMAS, ABRAHAM, a poor Jew, was granted a pass to travel from England to Holland, 23 October 1706. [TNA.SP44.393.181]

CALLAS, MOSES, in St Kitts, 1712. [JTP.1712.393]

CAMBERG, LOUIS, born 1850, died 15 February 1917. [Newington MI, Edinburgh]

CAMPANELL, DANIELL, a militiaman in Barbados, 1679. [TNA.CO1.44.47]

CAMPANELL, MORDECAY, from Barbados aboard the ketch Swallow bound for New England in 1679. [TNA.CO1]

CAPADOCIA, MOSES, with his wife **Abigail**, daughter **Rachel,** and son **David,** in the parish of St James, Duke's Place, London, 1695. [LRS. 1966.52]

CARA, JOSEPH, a Jew, was granted a pass to travel from England to Holland, 23 July 1706. [TNA.SP44.393.36]

CARACOSA, LEON, an alien, was granted denization, 13 May 1700. [Patent Roll, 12 William III, part 4]

CARCAS, RECHEL, a poor Jew, was granted a pass to travel from England to Holland, 10 October 1706. [TNA.SP44.393.178]

CARDAZO, ABRAHAM, probate 1791 PCC. [TNA]

CARDOZO, MOSSEH YESURUN, 'born beyond the sea', a grant of denization, 15 April 1672. [Patent Roll, 24 Car ii, part 4]

CARDOZO, SAMUEL, Member of the Royal College of Surgeons, London, graduated MD from King's College, Aberdeen, on 15 April 1859. [KCA. 173]

CARE, SAMUEL, a Jew, was granted a pass to travel from England to Holland, 23 July 1706. [TNA.SP44.393.36]

CARELES, ISAAC, was granted a pass to travel from England to Holland on 6 April 1705. [TNA.SP44.390.417]

CARREROE, ABRAHAM, with his wife **Sarah,** and daughter **Rebecca,** in the parish of All Hallows, London Wall, 1695. [LRS.1966.54]

CARVAJAL, ABRAHAM ISRAEL, a petitioner in London, 1658. [SPDom.Commonwealth.cxxv.58]

CARVAJAL, ANTONIO FERNANDO, from Fundoa, Lower Beira, Portugal, and his sons **Alonso Jorge Carvajal** and **Joseph Ferdinando Carvajal,** merchants in Leadenhall Street, London, and the Canary Islands, having lived in England for over 20 years, were granted a patent of denization by Oliver Cromwell on 17 August 1655. He died in November 1659 as chief of the Marrano Congregation in Creechurch Lane, London. [TJS.ii.45][Patent Roll, 1655, part 4]

CASEN, HEZEKIA, a surgeon and a gentleman, with his wife **Sasilva,** in the parish of St Faith under St Paul's, London, 1695. [LRS.1966.55]

CASRIL, MARCUS, a hatter and furrier, 17 Market Place, Hull, Yorkshire, 1848. [HCA]

CASTELO, DAVID, an alien, was granted denization, 9 March 1694. [Patent Roll, 6 William and Mary, pt.1. S.P.Dom. Warrant book 38.496]

CHACON, AUGUSTINE CORONEL, in London, 1652. [TJS.i.70] [Cal.SPDom.1654.448]

CHAEL, JACOB M., born 1835, died 7 October 1896. [Newington MI, Edinburgh]

CHAFE, SOLOMON, a planter in St Peter's parish, Barbados, 1679. [TNA.CO1.44.47]

CHAPMAN, ABRAHAM, a merchant in Amsterdam, Holland, was permitted to settle with his family and goods in England, 1673. [SPDom.1673.529]

CHAVIES, ABIGAIL, in the parish of All Hallows, London Wall, 1695. [LRS.1966.59]

CHAVIES, HESTER, in the parish of All Hallows, London Wall, 1695. [LRS.1966.59]

CHAVIES, RACHEL, in the parish of All Hallows, London Wall, 1695. [LRS.1966.59]

CHESARKIE, LEAH, born 1836, died 1 April 1920. [Piershill MI, Edinburgh]

CHESARKIE, LEIB, born 1831, died 11 August 1907, father of Arthur. [Piershill MI, Edinburgh]

CHEVUS, BENJAMIN, on Nevis, 1708. [TNA.CO152-157]

CHEZECK, ABELL, an apprentice, in the parish of St Mary, Aldermary, London, 1695. [LRS.1966.61]

CHILLON, DAVID, a militiaman in Barbados, 1679. [TNA.CO1.44.47]

CHILLON, ISAK LOPES, a petitioner in London, 1658. [SPDom.Commonwealth.cxxv.58]

CHOLLET, ABRAHAM LOUIS, in Charleston, USA, brother of Isaac Henry Chollet in Maudon, Switzerland, probate 1821, PCC. [TNA]

COEN, AARON, with his wife **Sarah**, in the parish of St Katharine Cree, London, 1695. [LRS.1966.66]

COENE, PETER, and his son **Peter Coene**, born in Holland, grants of denization, 17 December 1661. [Patent Roll, 13 Car 23]

COHEN, ABRAHAM, in Jamaica, 1665. [SPAWI.1665.948/949]

COHEN, ABRAHAM JACOB, an alien, a grant of denization, in April 1670. [Patent Roll, 22 Car ii]

COHEN, ABRAHAM, born 1841, died 23 October 1926. [Newington MI, Edinburgh]

COHEN, ANDREW, died in Jamaica during 1790. [GM.60.1214]

COHEN, ARTHUR, matriculated at Magdalene College, Cambridge, graduated BA in 1858.

COHEN, BARNETT A., in Bristol, 1793. [Bristol Directory, 1793/1794]

COHEN, BENJAMIN, born 1814 in Norwich, a dealer, Nicolson Street, Edinburgh, 1851. [Census]

COHEN, CAROLINE, born 1828 in England, a traveller's wife, 57 Stockwell Street, Glasgow, with sons **Samuel Cohen**, born 1844 in England, and **Michael Cohen**, born 1850 in England, 1841. [Census]

COHEN, DANIEL, an alien, was granted denization, 12 April 1700. [Patent Roll, 12 William III, part 4]

COHEN, DAVID, graduated MD in Aberdeen, 1755. [CJ]

COHEN, DAVID, born 'in foreign parts' 1786, in Newcastle-upon-Tyne, Northumberland, 1832-1835. [NRS.NRAS4276.3.16]; optician, 4 Collingwood Street, Newcastle-upon-Tyne, 1820; 1823; husband of **Esther**.... born 1786 'in foreign parts', residing in Grey Street, Newcastle upon Tyne, 1841. [Census][CDS][Newcastle Directory][SNE]

COHEN, DOUGLAS, from Wales, graduated MD from Edinburgh University in 1828. [EMG.84]

COHEN, EMANUEL, born 1823 in England, a stationer, 105 Stockwell Street, Glasgow, 1851. [Census]

COHEN,[later PALGRAVE] FRANCIS EPHRAIM, born 1788 in London, son of **Meyer Cohen** and his wife **Rachel Levien**, a historian, died 6 July 1861.

COHEN, FRANCIS, Temple, London, a plan for publication, 25 April 1822. [NRS.RH9.17.240]

COHEN, HENRY, born 1815 in London, a 'fuse maker', 11 Calton Street, Leith, 1851. [Census]

COHEN, HYMEN, 1819, reference in **David Wolfe's** deed. [NRS.RD5.193.713]

COHEN, ISAAC, from Manchester, a hatter in Glasgow, was admitted as a burgess and freeman of the city on 22 September 1812. [GBR]

COHEN, ISAAC, born 1828, died 16 April 1897. [Newington MI, Edinburgh]

COHEN, ISAAC, born 1831 in Germany, a clothier's assistant, 6 Miller Street, Glasgow, 1851. [Census]

COHEN, JACOB, a poor Jew, was granted a pass to travel from England to Holland, 10 October 1706. [TNA.SP44.393.172]

COHEN, JACOB ARON, in Jermyn Street, Westminster, London, late of South Carolina, probate 1813, PCC. [TNA]

COHEN, JOSEPH, a German Jew, was granted a pass to travel from England to Holland, 5 April 1706. [TNA.SP44.390.415a]

COHEN, JOSEPH, aged 27, a tailor, his spouse **Sarah Cohen**, aged 24, a tailoress, 24 Waterloo Place, Bristol. [1841 Census]; an assignment, 1843. [BRO.3394.1H]

COHEN, JOSEPH, born 1811 in Germany, a merchant, 78 Stockwell Street, Glasgow, 1851, with his wife **Rachel Cohen**, born 1813 in England, son **Merrie Cohen**, born 1836 in England, daughter **Trasy Cohen**, born 1839 in England, daughter **Helen Cohen**, born 1841 in England, son **Solomon Cohen**, born 1845 in Glasgow, and daughter **Sarah Cohen**, born 1849 in Glasgow. [Census]; schochet, reader and teacher of the Old Hebrew Congregation in Glasgow before 1846, thereafter a wholesale tobacco merchant. [SCJ.23][Jewish Chronicle, 4 September 1846]

COHEN, JUDAH, 1819, reference in David Wolfe's deed. [NRS.RD5.193.713]

COHEN, JUDAH HYMEN, Grand Parade, St Leonards-on-Sea, died 20 April 1855, inventory 1855, Commissariat of Edinburgh. [NRS]

COHEN, JULES, born 1827 in Prussia, a wholesale traveller, 21 Stockwell Place, Glasgow, 1851. [Census]

COHEN, LASER, a German Jew, was granted a pass to travel from England to Holland, 24 May 1706. [TNA.SP44.390.458]

COHEN, LAZER, a German Jew, was granted a pass to travel from England to Holland, 12 June 1706. [TNA.SP44.393.6]

COHEN, LEVI, a German Jew, was granted a pass to travel from England to Holland, 11 April 1706. [TNA.SP44.390.422]

COHEN, LEVI, a poor Jew, was granted a pass to travel from England to Holland, 21 October 1706. [TNA.SP44.393.179]

COHEN, LEVI, a Scottish Admiralty Court decreet, 1778. [NRS.AC8.2022]

COHEN, MARCUS, born 1806 in Prussia, at 14 Well Street, Glasgow, in 1851. [Census]

COHEN, MORRIS, a jeweller and goldsmith, 5 Myltongate, Hull, Yorkshire, 1852. [HCA]

COHEN, MOSES, a dealer in gold and silver in Bristol, 1757 . [prosecuted as trading though not a burgess].[BRO]

COHEN, MOSES, a color maker in Bristol, 1761. [BRO.00401.59]

COHEN, Reverend RAPHAEL ISAAC, born 1803 in Poland, died 1865 in Dover, Kent. [Deane Road Cemetery, Liverpool]

COHEN, REBECCA, born 1843, died 28 August 1915. [Newington MI, Edinburgh]

COHEN, S. P., president of the Old Hebrew Congregation in Glasgow, 1849. [SCJ.23]

COHEN, SALOMON S., born 1805, died 15 September 1870. [Newington MI, Edinburgh]

COHEN, SIMON, born 1803 in Prussia, a teacher of Hebrew, 82 George Street, Glasgow, 1851. [Census]

COHEN, SIMON M., born 1806 in Devon, an optician of 12 Royal Terrace, Glasgow, with his wife **Harriet Cohen,** born 1806 in Devon, son **Levin H. C. Cohen,** born 1843 in Glasgow, **Katherine Cohen,** born 1846 in Glasgow, **Benjamin Cohen,** born 1848 in Glasgow, 1851. [Census]

COHEN, SIMON, born 1806 'in foreign parts', a teacher, 15 South College Street, Edinburgh, 1841. [Census]

COHEN, SIMON BENJAMIN, jeweller and general dealer, 9 Leith Street Terrace, Edinburgh, 1859. [ELD]

COHEN, SOLOMON, born 1806 in Prussia, a travelling dealer, a visitor at 140 Rose Street, Edinburgh, 1851. [Census]

COHEN, SOLOMON, dealer in watches and watch materials, 5 Leith Street Terrace, Edinburgh, 1859. [ELD]

COHEN, URIA, a German Jew, was granted a pass to travel from England to Holland, 5 April 1706. [TNA.SP44.390.415a]

COHEN, ..., born in Berlin, advertised a sculpture for sale in Edinburgh on 8 May 1777. [NRS.GD113.3.1383]

COHEN, ..., in Dundee, Angus, 1813. [NRS.CS234.C14.6]

COHEN, ..., 1836. [NRS.CS236A.20.4]

COHEN and LEVY, a Scottish Admiralty Court decreet, 1778. [NRS.AC8.2022]

COHENS, ..., partner in **A. Harris, Cohens & Co.** watchmakers in Glasgow, 1850. [Glasgow Directory]

COHNERT, M., jeweller and goldsmith, 10 Leith Street, Edinburgh, 1849. [EPOD]

COIN, BARUCH, a German Jew, was granted a pass to travel from England to Holland, 14 May 1706. [TNA.SP44.390.451]

COLLIER, BENJAMIN, with his wife **Hannah,** and son **Joseph,** in the parish of St Andrew Undershaft, London, 1695. [LRS.1966.68]

COLLUE, ABRAHAM, aged 19, a weaver from Stepney, London, an indentured servant bound from London to Maryland in 1725. [CLRO]

CONTINHO, ISAAC PERERA, an alien, a grant of denization, 14 December 1666, [Patent Roll, 18 Car ii]; a free denizen of Barbados, 1669. [ActsPCCol.I.534]

COUTINHO, MOSES, an alien, was granted denization, 9 March 1694. [Patent Roll, 6 William and Mary, pt.1. S.P.D. Warrant book 38.496]

COPPEL, JANE, born 1729, a nurse from Manchester, emigrated from Liverpool aboard the York Packet bound for New York in 1774. [TNA.T47.9/11]

COPPELL, SUSANNA, widow and executrix of William Coppell of Kingston, Jamaica, a deed, 1788. [Car.2.331]

CORA, AARON, a German Jew, was granted a pass to travel from England to Holland, 31 May 1706. [TNA.SP44.390.461]

CORDIOX, JACOB, a militiaman in Barbados, 1679. [TNA.CO1.44.47]

CORDOSO, ISAACK, with his wife **Judith,** and son **David,** in the parish of St James, Duke's Place, London, 1695. [LRS.1966.72]

CORDOSO, MOSES NUNES, with his wife **Rachel,** daughters **Hester, Sarah, Rachel,** and **Rebecca,** and son **Abraham,** in the parish of St James, Duke's Place, London, 1695. [LRS.1966.72]

CORDOZA, SOLOMON, an alien, residing in Barbados, a grant of denization, 29 May 1663. [Patent Roll, 15 Car ii.10]; in St Michael's parish, Barbados, 1679. [TNA.CO1.44.47]; with 3 children {?} in St Michael's 1680. [TNA.CO1]

CORERO, ANTONY, a merchant, with his wife **Rebecca,** sons **David, Aaron, Solomon,** and daughters **Rachel, Sarah,** and **Deborah,** in the parish of St James, Duke's Place, London, 1695. [LRS.1966.72]

CORSELLUS, ISAACK, a militiaman in Barbados, 1679. [TNA.CO1.44.47]

COSS, KEVA, a Jew, was granted a pass to travel from England to Holland, 2 May 1706. [TNA.SP44.390.445]

COSTANIO, ABRAHAM, in St Michael's parish, Barbados, 1679. [TNA.CO1.44.47]

COTINHO, MOSES HENRIQUES, an indentured servant from Barbados aboard the Adventure, master Edward Duffield, bound for Jamaica, in November 1679. [TNA.CO1.44.47]

COUEN, JACOB, born in Borscheit, Germany, son of Simon Couen and his wife Getrow, a grant of naturalisation, 1693. [Naturalisation Act, 4 and 5, William and Mary, 39]

COULONE, MOSES, in the parish of St Dunstan in the East, London, 1695. [LRS.1966.74]

COUTINHO, DANIEL, born in 1658 at Villa Flora, Portugal, an English subject and a merchant in Creechurch Lane, London, also book-keeper to Francis de Cassares, a witness before the High Court of the Admiralty of England in 1698. [TNA.HCA.Exams., Vol.81]

COUTTINHO, DAVID, an alien, a grant of denization, 13 January 1696. [Patent Roll, 7 Wm. iii, part 4]

COUTTINHO, ISAAC, an alien, a grant of denization, 13 January 1696. [Patent Roll, 7 Wm. iii, part 4]

COUTY, RABBA, a burgher of New York and a merchant trading to Barbados, 1671, his ketch, the Trial and its cargo, was seized in Jamaica in 1672. [SPAWI.1672.968.ii/iii/iv; 999]

COWEN, HANNAH, born 1844, died 1 June 1913. [Piershill MI, Edinburgh]

CRAYESTEIN, ABRAHAM, a merchant, with his wife **Rebecca**, and daughter **Mary**, in the parish of St Lawrence Poultrey, London, 1695. [LRS.1966.76]

CRONINGSBURG, DAVID, a German Jew, was granted a pass to travel from England to Holland, 25 September 1706. [TNA.SP44.393.99]

CRONINGSBURG, JACOB, a German Jew, was granted a pass to travel from England to Holland, 25 September 1706. [TNA.SP44.393.99]

CRONENBERG, WILLIAM, from the West Indies, graduated MD from Edinburgh University in 1822. [EMG.67]

CUNHA, DANIEL MENDES, probate 1789 PCC. [TNA]

CURTANEZ, JACOB, a bachelor in the parish of St James, Duke's Place, London, 1695. [LRS.1966.79]

CURTENICA, PERERO, a bachelor, in the parish of St James, Duke's Place, London, 1695. [LRS.1966.79]

D'ALMANZA, MANUEL, letters of denization, 16 July 1689. [CalSPDom. 1689.188]

DA COSTA, ANTHONY, a merchant in London, a grant of denization, 27 August 1684. [Patent Roll, 36 Car ii, part 6]

DA COSTA, ANTONIO, 'born beyond the seas', a grant of denization, 19 March 1688. [4 Jas ii, part 6]

DA COSTA, DANIEL MENDES, in Jamaica, probate 1755, PCC. [TNA]

DA COSTA, DAVID, in London, 1648. [Cal.SPDom]; born in foreign parts, residing in Barbados, a grant of denization, 8 Mar 1663. [Patent Roll, 15 Car ii.20]

DA COSTA, ISAAC, in the parish of St Helen, London, 1695. [LRS. 1966.80]

DA COSTA, ISAAC MENDES, in Jamaica, probate 1766, PCC. [TNA]

DA COSTA, ISAAC, a soldier during the French and Indian Wars, a Loyalist in 1776. [TNA.AO12.99.218; 13.44.12]

DA COSTA, ISAAC RODRIGUEZ, in Jamaica, probate 1805, PCC. [TNA]

DA COSTA, JOSEPH NUNES, an alien, a grant of denization, 1 June 1688. [Patent Roll, 4 Jas II, part 6]

DA COSTA, Lady REBECCA MENDES, probate 1792 PCC. [TNA]

DA COSTA, REBECCA MENDES, in Jamaica, probate 1804, PCC. [TNA]

DA COVER, DAVID, took the Oath of Association in New York, 1696. [TNA]

DA CUNHA, JOSEPH, graduated MD in Aberdeen, 1814. [CJ]

D'AGUILAR, BENJAMIN, in Jamaica, probate 1813, PCC. [TNA]

D'AGUILAR, REBECCA, in Jamaica, probate 1810, PCC. [TNA]

DANIEL, HENRY, a glass cutter and engraver in Edinburgh, and his spouse **Rose Nathan**, process of divorce, 1790. [NRS.CC8.6.853]

DANIEL, JOSEPH, from the island of Nevis, graduated MD from Edinburgh University, 1809. [EMG.41]

DANIEL, JOSEPH, a decreet, 4 August 1830. [NRS.SC.Midlothian#195]

DANIEL, MOSES, born 1730 in Hanover, Germany, settled in Edinburgh by 1787, a spectacle maker. [FJC.5/36][EBR:SL115]

DANIEL, PHINEAS, a writer in Edinburgh in 1813/1816/1825/1828/1830/1832. [FJC.36][NRS.CS36.7.65; B59.34.122/128; CS237.D9.34; CS46.1830.2.136; CS44.93.49]

DARNIN, REBECCA, a German Jew, was granted a pass to travel from England to Holland, 18 May 1706. [TNA.SP44.390.453]

DA SILVA, RALPH VAS, a merchant of Crutched Friars, London, a contract, 1776. [Car.3.157]

DA VEIGA, SAMUEL B., in Jamaica, probate 1812, PCC. [TNA]

DAVEIGAR, SAMUEL, 'born in foreign parts', a grant of denization, 2 August 1661. [Patent Roll, 13 Car ii.17]

DAVIDS, EMANUEL, a German Jew, was granted a pass to travel from England to Holland, 12 August 1706. [TNA.SP44.393.57]

DAVID, GABRIEL, aged 51, born in Amsterdam, a merchant in Edinburgh by 1804. [EBR.SL115]

DAVID, ISAAC, a German Jew, was granted a pass to travel from England to Holland, 29 March 1706. [TNA.SP44.390.409]

DAVID, JOSUE, took the Oath of Association in New York, 1696. [TNA]

DAVID, SAMUEL, a German Jew, was granted a pass to travel from England to Holland, 30 April 1706. [TNA.SP44.390.443]

DAVIDSON, JONAH, born 1835, died 26 March 1892. [Newington MI, Edinburgh]

DAVIS, ANNA, born in England 1823, a governess, 36 Hanover Street, Edinburgh, in 1851, died 10 January 1857. [JBGE][Census][Braid Place MI, Edinburgh]

DAVIS, BERNARD, born 1827 in England, a clothier's traveller, 6 Miller Street, Glasgow, 1851. [Census]

DAVIES, DAVID, an optician in Glasgow, father of Edward Davies, 1824; of the George Street Synagogue, 1840s. [SCJ.19/22]

DAVIS, DAVID, a jeweller in Glasgow, by 1850. [SCHR.111.206]

DAVIS, EDWARD, a tailor 16 High Street, Edinburgh, 1819-1826. [FJC. 36]

DAVIS, HENRY JACOB GORDON, died 4 May 1861 aged 17 months. [JBGE]

DAVIS, LION, born 1757, from Amsterdam, Holland, landed in Margate, Kent, settled in Edinburgh by 1798, husband of **Sarah** and father of **Sally**; by 1812 he was an umbrella and leather cape maker at 87 Canongate, Edinburgh. [FJC.5/35][EBR:SL115]

DAVIS, JAMES, tailor, 134 High Street, Edinburgh, 1821; in 1840 he was "sec. and cal-master, Tailor's house of call at 11 Warriston Close", Edinburgh. [FJC.36]

DAVIS, MARIA, born 1791 in England, a visitor/aunt at 36 Hanover Street, Edinburgh, 1851. [Census]

DAVIS, PHILIP, born in Dublin, Ireland, 1811, a patent medicine vendor, 72 Great King Street, Edinburgh, 1840, 36 Hanover Street, Edinburgh, 1851, wife **Eve,** born 1817 in England, daughter **Phoebe** born 1847 in Glasgow, daughter **Maria,** born 1851 in Edinburgh. [FJC.36][Census]

DAVIS, SAMUEL, of the George Street Synagogue, Glasgow, 1840s. [SCJ.22]

DE ANDRADE, LUYS, an alien, a grant of denization, 9 June 1688. [Patent Roll, 4 Jas ii, part 6]

DE BRITO, ABRAHAM ISRAEL, a petitioner in London, 1658. [SPDom.Commonwealth.cxxv.58]

DECHAUIS, SAMUEL, in St Michael's parish, Barbados, 1679. [TNA.CO1.44.47]; with 2 children{?} in St Michael's 1680. [TNA.CO1]

DE CASERES, B., petitioned the Queen of Sweden, [Rawl.mss.A26, fo. 388];a Jewish merchant [and two others] with a recommendation by the King of Denmark, was licensed to reside in Barbados on 24 July 1661. [SPAWI.1661.140]

DE CACERES, JAHACOB, a petitioner in London, 1658. [SPDom.Commonwealth.cxxv.58]

DE CASARES, FRANCISCO, an alien, a grant of denization, 30 November 1693. [Patent Roll, 5 William and Mary 4, part 2]; **Francis de Cassares,** on trial before the High Court of the Admiralty of England in 1698. [TNA.HCA.Vol.81.1698]

DE CASERES, SIMON, proposed to revictual and fortify Jamaica, 1650s. [Rawl.mss.A30.fo.299][TJS.iii.97]

DE CASTER, ISAAC, with his wife **Rachel,** and son **Joseph,** in the parish of St Andrew Undershaft, London, 1695. [LRS.1966.86]

DE CASTER, SAMUEL, a bachelor, in the parish of St Andrew Undershaft, London, 1695. [LRS.1966.86]

DE CASTOR, SOLOMON, a widower, in the parish of St Katherine Cree, London, 1695. [LRS.1966.86]

DE CASTRO, BEATRIZ, a widow, with **Rachel,** a widow, and their children **Rebecca, Isaack,** and **Abraham,** in the parish of St James, Duke's Place, London, 1695. [LRS.1966.86]

DE CASTRO, JACOB, deceased, executor of **Jacob Mendez Gutturez** a merchant in Jamaica, 1739. [ActsPCCol.III.645]

DE CASTROS, MOSES, a bachelor, in the parish of St Andrew Undershaft, London, 1695. [LRS.1966.86]

DE CASTRO, JUDITH, widow of **Moses Lamera,** a petitioner in Jamaica, 1752. [ActsPCCol.1745-1766.151]

DE CHAVIS, SAMUEL, a militiaman in Barbados, 1679. [TNA.CO1.44.47]

DE COMPAS, Mrs LEAH, in St Michael's parish, Barbados, 1679. [TNA.CO1.44.47]; with 3 children {?} in St Michael's 1680. [TNA.CO1]

DA COSTA, ALUARO, born in Lisbon, Portugal, son of **Fernando Mendes Da Costa,** a grant of naturalisation, 1667. [Patent Roll, 19 Car ii.9]

DA COSTA, ANTHONY, a merchant in London, a grant of denization, 27 August 1684. [Patent Roll, 36 Car ii, part 6]

DA COSTA, DANIEL MENDES, a petitioner in Jamaica, 1752. [ActsPCCol. 1745-1766.151]

DA COSTO, DAVID, a planter in St Thomas's parish, Barbados, 1679. [TNA.CO1.44.47]

DE COSTA, DAVID, a cavalryman of the Leeward Regiment, 1679. [TNA.CO1.44.47]

DA COSTA, ISAAC, a soldier during the French and Indian War, 1755-1763, a landowner in Massachusetts, a Loyalist claim in 1783. [TNA.AO12.99.218, etc]

DE COSTA, JOHN MENDES, a merchant in London, alleged to have contravened the Navigation Acts, 1697. [CTP.XLIV.69]

DA COSTA, JOHN, merchant in London, applied for a land grant in America, 1734. [SPAWI.XLI.9/242]

DE COSTA, JOSEPH, with his wife **Leah,** in the parish of All Hallows, London Wall, 1695. [LRS.1966.86]

DA COSTA, MOSES MENDES, born 1780, died in Barbados on 8 November 1845, [GM.NS24.665]

DE FONSECA, ALONSO, servant of Antonio Fernandes Caravajal merchant in London, granted a pass to travel to Flanders, 30 March 1655. [SPDom.1655.580]

DE FONSEQUA, JACOB, a planter in St Peter's parish, Barbados, 1679. [TNA.CO1.44.47]

DE FRIES, Mrs ROSETTA, born in Amsterdam, Holland, in 1778, died in Edinburgh 13 December 1869, grandmother of **Henry, Esther, Israel** and **Rose Levy.** [Newington MI, Edinburgh]

DEHN, ISRAEL, and Company, decreet of absolvitor, 1825. [NRS.CS44.94.37]

DE LA CERDA, DOMINGO, a petitioner in London, 1658; an alien, a grant of denization, 10 June 1675.[SPDom.Commonwealth.cxxv.58] [Patent Roll, 27 Car ii part 8]

DE LA COSTA, BENTO, in London 1655. [CalSPDom.1655.137]

DE LA LOYHOY, PHIL., a witness, London, 1656. [Cal. SPDom. 1656.105/iv]

DE LA PARR, ISAAC, an overseer, was transported from Surinam aboard the <u>Hercules</u> to Jamaica in 1675. [SPAWI.1675.675.vii]

DE LA PENHA, ISAAC, a merchant in Barbados, an alien, was granted denization, 3 June 1699. [Patent Roll, 11 William III, pt.2.]

DE LA PAXA, ISAAC, a Jew in Surinam petitioned to go to Jamaica, 1676. [SPAWI.1676.818.i]

DE LA SELLA, DOMINGO, a Spanish Jew, a witness in London, 1656. [Cal.SPDom.cvxxvi.1656]

DELCANO, MOSES, with his wife Judith, daughters Sarah, Hester, and sons Joseph, Mordecai, in the parish of St James, Duke's Place, London, 1695. [LRS.1966.86]

DE LEAO, or DE LIJOU, BENJAMIN PEREYRA, an alien, a grant of denization, 10 December 1695. [Patent Roll, 7 Wm. iii, part 4]

DE LEON, DAVID, trading with McNeil, Sadler & Claxton in St Kitts, 1760. [NRS.CS96.4370]

DE LIMA, HAIM ABINUM, a merchant in Nevis, 'but now at Mrs Judith Dias house in the Minories, London [died in parish of St Botolph, Aldgate, London', probate 1765 PCC. [TNA]. His will refers to his wife Rebecca Abinum de Lima of Curacao, his niece Sarah, daughter of Elias Burgos in Barbados, his kinsman Jacob, son of his uncle David de Piza, Haim son of his kinsman Mordecay Abinum de Lima, to his kinswoman Haim Abinum de Lima, Isaac Pardo merchant in Curacao, to Rachael, Clara and Judith daughters of his kinsman Mordecay Abinum de Lima in Curacao, to kinsman Jacob, son of uncle David de Piza, to friend David de Leon merchant on St Kitts, to kinsman Abraham, son of uncle David de Piza. Attornies were Moses Nunes the elder of St Catherine Cree, London, Isaac Israel Nunes of All Hallows on the Wall, London.

DE LION, DAVID, a militiaman in Barbados, 1679. [TNA.CO1.44.47]

DE LION, DAVID, in St Kitts, executor of Haim de Lima of Nevis, 1765. [TNA]

DE LION, SAMPSON, a militiaman in Barbados, 1679. [TNA.CO1.44.47]

DE LIZ, ESTHER, was granted a pass to travel from England to Holland on 6 April 1705. [TNA.SP44.390.417]

DELMAR, JACOB, in Jamaica, probate 1790, PCC. [TNA]

DELPRATT, JOSEPH, in Kingston, Jamaica, a covenant, 1796. [Car. 2.331]

DELPRATT, SAMUEL, in Kingston, Jamaica, a covenant, 1796. [Car. 2.331]

DE LYON, MOSIAS, a planter in St Peter's parish, Barbados, 1679. [TNA.CO1.44.47]

DE MARCADO, ABRAHAM, an alien, a grant of denization, 11 October 1687. [Patent Roll, 1 Jas ii]

DI MEDINA, DIEGO, born in Bordeaux, France, a merchant in London, a grant of denization, 23 December 1672. [Patent Roll, 24 Car ii, part 4]

DE MEDINA, JACOB, an alien, was granted denization 14 December 1694. [S.P.Dom.Warrant book.39.124]; a militiaman in Barbados, 1679. [TNA.CO1.44.47]

DE MERCADO, DAVID RAPHAEL, 'born beyond the seas', a merchant in Barbados, a grant of denization, 11 July 1678. [Patent Roll, 30 Car ii. 1]; in St Michael's parish, Barbados, 1679. [TNA.CO1.44.47]; with 3 children {?} in St Michael's 1680. [TNA.CO1]

DE MERCADO, KIAUH, petitioned to emigrate to the Plantations, 1680. [SPAWI.1680.1347]; Moses Kiaugh de Mercado, a physician and an alien, a grant of denization, in January 1680. [Patent Roll, 31 Car ii]

DE MESQUITA, ABRAHAM BUENO, an alien, was granted denization 2 February 1695. [S.P.Dom.Warrant book.40.16]; on Nevis 1708, [TNA.CO152-157]; resettled on Nevis, 1712. [JTP.1709-1715.383]

DE MESQUITA, BENJAMIN BUENO, an alien, a grant of denization 24 October 1664. [Patent Roll, 16 Car ii]; a Jew in Jamaica, with his sons Abraham Cohen and Jacob Ulhuo, 1665. [SPAWI.1665.949];

DE MESQUITA, REBECCA HENRIQUES, in Jamaica, probate 1798, PCC. [TNA]

DE MIRANDA, JERONIMO FERNANDEZ, born in Bordeaux, France, a merchant in London, a grant of denization, 23 December 1672. [Patent Roll, 24 Car ii. 4]

DE PASS, ABRAHAM DANIEL, fourth son of Daniel de Pass in London, married Judith Lazarus, eldest daughter of Abraham Lazarus, in Kingston, Jamaica, on 8 July 1846. [GM.NS26.418]

DE PAIVA, ABRAHAM, 'born beyond the seas', a grant of denization, 19 March 1688. [4 Jas ii, part 6]

DE PEIZA, ISAAC, a merchant in Barbados, 1741. [ActsPCCol.III.698]

DE PINTO, JACOB, was granted a pass to travel from England to Holland on 6 April 1705. [TNA.SP44.390.417]

DE PIZA, DAVID, a gentleman in Barbados, executor of Haim de Lima in Nevis, 1765. [TNA]

DE PISO, AARON ISRAEL, a Jew in Barbados, 1665. [SPAWI.1665.948]

DE PISO, ISAAC ISRAEL, a Jew in Barbados, 1665. [SPAWI.1665.948]

DE PISO, MOSES, a Jew in Barbados, 1665. [SPAWI.1665.948]

DE PIVER, ABRAHAM, with his wife **Sarah,** sons **Moses, Isaac, Jacob, Aaron, David,** and daughters **Laer, Judith, Esther,** in the parish of St Katherine Cree, London, 1695. [LRS.1966.87]

DE PORTO, ANTONIO, a petitioner in London, 1658. [SPDom.Commonwealth.cxxv.58]

DE PORTO, SARAH, a widow, with son **Joseph,** and daughters **Judith, Deborah,** in the parish of St Katherine Cree, London, 1695. [LRS. 1966.87]

DE PRADOE, ISAAC, a Jew in Surinam petitioned to go to Jamaica, 1676. [SPAWI.1676.818.i]

DERKHEIM, MOSES MYER, in Norfolk, Virginia, probate 1817, PCC. [TNA]

DE SAVIDO, MOSES, in St Michael's parish, Barbados, 1679. [TNA.CO1.44.47]; with 5 children {?} in St Michael's 1680. [TNA.CO1]

DESAY, JACOB, with his wife **Rachel,** in the parish of St James, Duke's Place, London, 1695. [LRS.1966.88]

DESAY, LEER, a widow, with son **Isaack,** in the parish of St James, Duke's Place, London, 1695. [LRS.1966.88]

DE SILVA, AARON, a grant of denization, 12 July 1661. [Patent Roll, 13 Car ii.17]

DE SILVA, AARON, was transported from Surinam aboard the Hercules to Jamaica in 1675. [SPAWI.1675.675.vii; 1676.825]

DE SILVER, ABRAHAM, a planter in St Peter's parish, Barbados, 1679. [TNA.CO1.44.47]

DESITRER, JUDITH, a widow, with son **Joshua,** daughters **Hannah,** and **Sarah,** in the parish of St Katherine Cree, London, 1695. [LRS.1966.88]

DE SOLIS, GABRIEL, from Surinam aboard the Hercules bound for Jamaica, 1675. [SPAWI.1675.675vii]

DE SOUZA, SIMON, a petitioner in London, 1658. [SPDom.Commonwealth.cxxv.58]

DE SYMONS, SAMUEL LYON, died in his residence, Cumberland Street, Portman Square, London, on 4 May 1860, aged 72. [GM.NS.VIII.644]

DE TORRES, JACOB, a merchant in Jamaica, a grant of denization, 25 May 1671. [Patent Roll, 23 Car ii part 5]

DE TOUAR, ABRAHAM, in London 16... [TJS.i.69]

DEUREDE, PAUL, with 2 children {?} in St Michael's 1680. [TNA.CO1]

DEUTCH, LEVI, aged 15, a laborer from Bristol, an indentured servant bound from Bristol to Maryland in 1774. [TNA.T47.9/11]

DE WOLF, STARR, a petition, 1848. [NRS.CS235.T.19.7]

DIAZ, ABRAHAM, the younger, testamentary trustee of Haim de Liza in Nevis, 1765. [TNA]

DIAS, ISAAC VERNANDES, an alien, was granted denization on 9 March 1694. [Patent Roll, 6 William and Mary, pt.1. S.P.D. Warrant book 38.496]

DIAS, JOEL, in Barbados, probate 1724 PCC. [TNA]

DIAS, JOSEPH, a German Jew, was granted a pass to travel from England to Holland, 7 August 1706. [TNA.SP44.393.52]

DIAS, LUIS, a free denizen of Barbados, 1669. [ActsPCCol.I.534]; in St Michael's parish, Barbados, 1679. [TNA.CO1.44.47]; with 6 children {?} in St Michael's 1680. [TNA.CO1]

DOLNIS, REBECCA ELIZABETH, born in Godens near Emden, Germany, daughter of Daniel Sachsius, and the wife of Abraham Dolnis a merchant in London, a grant of naturalisation, 1677. [Patent Roll, 29 Car ii.20]

DORMIDO, MANUEL MARTINEZ, [alias **David Abrabanel**], born in Andalusia, Spain, petitioned in 1649 for the repeal of the Act banishing Jews from England; a merchant in London, petitioned to be denizised, 1677. Father of **Solomon** and **Aron.** [TJS.i.70; iii.87][SPAWI.1677. 556]

DORMEDO, SOLOMON, with his wife, in the parish of St Andrew Undershaft, London, 1695. [LRS.1966.91]

DRAGONER, ISAAC, a German Jew, was granted a pass to travel from England to Holland, 25 September 1706. [TNA.SP44.393.100]

DUARTE, JOSEPH PEREIRA, an alien, was granted denization, 13 May 1700. [Patent Roll, 12 William III, part 4]

DUEREDE, PAUL, in St Michael's parish, Barbados, 1679. [TNA.CO1.44.47]

DURLACHER, ABRAHAM, born 1754 'in foreign parts', residing in Cheltenham, 1841. [Census]

DUTALL, JACOB, an alien, was granted denization, 12 April 1700. [Patent Roll, 12 William III, part 4]

EBEL, EDWARD, born 1801 'in foreign parts', a merchant, 131 Murraygate, house Victoria Square, later 44 Nethergate, Dundee, 1840; 1841. [DD][Census]

EDERSHEIM, ALFRED, born 1825 in Vienna, settled in Aberdeen, a Christian convert by 1849. [CJ.19]

ELIZER, ISAAC, in Rhode Island, 1765. [ActsPCCol.IV.716]

ELKANA, LEVI, a German Jew, was granted a pass to travel from England to Holland, 2 August 1706. [TNA.SP44.393.46]

EMANUEL, E., a furrier and cap-maker, 129 High Street, Edinburgh, 1840. [FJC.36]

EMANUEL, FRANCES, born 1806 'in foreign parts', a furrier, Bishop's Close, 129 High Street, Edinburgh, with **Rachel Emanuel,** born 1821 'in foreign parts', **Hymen Emanuel,** born 1834 in England, **Baroney Emanuel,** born 1838 in Edinburgh, **Lewis Emanuel,** born 1839, 1841. [Census]

EMANUEL, JOHN, born 1801 in Scotland, in Kirkintilloch, 1841. [Census]

ENNDE, CHARLES, born 1826 in Hamburg, a merchant, 111 Nethergate, Dundee, 1851. [Census]

ENRIQUES, DANIEL BUENO, a Portuguese, was granted denization, 5 September 1662. [Patent Roll, 14 Car. Ii.2]

ENRIQUES, JACOB JEOSA BUENEO, a Jamaican Jew, petitioned King Charles II for a licence to work a copper mine in Jamaica in 1661, and to use Jewish law and hold synagogues. [SPAWI.1661.138]

ENRIQUES, JOSEF BUENEO, a Jamaican Jew, petitioned King Charles II in 1661, for authority to use Jewish law and hold synagogues. [SPAWI. 1661.138]

ENRIQUES, MOISE BUENEO, a Jamaican Jew, petitioned King Charles II in 1661. [SPAWI.1661.138]

ENRIQUES, MOSE HENGAS, a merchant 'born in foreign parts', a grant of denization, 18 April 1664. [Patent Roll, 16 Car ii part 3]

ERGAS, ABRAHAM GOMES, a physician, died in Bath, 1786.

ESPINOSA, ABRAHAM, 'born beyond the seas', a merchant in Jamaica, a grant of denization, 3 July 1671. [Patent Roll, 23 Car ii part 5]

ESWALDER, ABRAHAM, was granted a pass to travel from England to Holland on 29 June 1706. [TNA.SP44.393.19]

EZEKIAL, MOSES, born 1776, by 1823 he was a sealing wax manufacturer at 5 Drummond Street, Edinburgh, with his home at 2 Adam Street, Edinburgh, he died 2 July 1850 [JBGE][FJC.37]

FACTOR, SARAH, born 1841, died 16 February 1898. [Newington MI, Edinburgh]

FARO, SALOMON GABAY, an alien, a grant of denization, 29 June 1668. [Patent Roll, 20 Car ii]

FEBURY, DANIEL, a German Jew, was granted a pass to travel from England to Holland, 12 June 1706. [TNA.SP44.393.5]

FERNANDES, ABRAHAM DIAS, a merchant, 1717. [JTP.1717.237]

FERNANDES, BENJAMIN DIAS, a merchant in Kingston, Jamaica, 1775, [Car.3.155] an executor, 1769. [ActsPCCol.V.118]

FERDINANDO, JACOB, in the parish of St James, Duke Place, London, 1695. [LRS.1966.105]

FERNANDEZ, DAVID, from Lambeth, London, died 1810 in St Thomas, West Indies. [GM.80.281]

FERNANDEZ, NUNO, an alien, a grant of denization, 9 June 1688. [Patent Roll, 4 Jas ii, part 6]

FERNANDES, SOLOMON DIAS, and his wife Sarah, 1788, he died 27 June 1791, she married Daniel Ximines 5 November 1795 and died on 23 June 1797, admin. 1797 PCC. [TNA][Car.2.368]

FEURTADO, JACOB, a merchant, an executor, 1769. [ActsPCCol.V.118]

FLATOW, SOLOMON, a stoneware merchant, 2 Dock Street, Leith, 1827. [FJC.37]

FONSECA, JACOB, in Jamaica, probate 1740, PCC. [TNA]

FONSECA, RACHEL, in Jamaica, probate 1807, PCC. [TNA]

FONTECO, JACOB, surgeon of His Majesty's Guards in the Caribee Islands, 1679. [TNA.CO1.44.47]

FORZON, SAMUEL, a merchant in Boston, Massachusetts, 1697. [TNA.HCA.Vol.81.Lopez v. Anthony]

FOUNZEKE, JACOB, a merchant in Barbados, a petition, 1681. [SPAWI. 1681.198]

FRANCIA, ABRAHAM, a bachelor, in the parish of St James, Duke Place, London, 1695. [LRS.1966.112]

FRANCIA, DOMINGO RODRIGUES, a petitioner in London, 1658; a grant of denization, 10 June 1675; he died in 1688, probate office, Exton, fo. 92. [SPDom.Commonwealth.cxxv.58][TJS.I.69][Patent Roll, 27 Car ii part 8]

FRANCIA, FRANCIS, an alien, a grant of denization, in February 1670. [Patent Roll, 22 Car. ii]

FRANCIA, ISAACK a bachelor, in the parish of St James, Duke Place, London, 1695. [LRS.1966.112]

FRANCIA, MINGO, in the parish of St Andrew Undershaft, London, 1695. [LRS.1966.112]

FRANCIA, MOSES, with his wife, and sons **Abraham** and **Isaac**, in the parish of St Andrew Undershaft, London, 1695. [LRS.1966.112]

FRANCIA, PETER, 'born beyond the seas', a grant of denization, 19 March 1688. [4 Jas ii, part 6]

FRANCIA, SYMON, born in Malaga, Spain, son of **George Francia**, a grant of naturalisation, 1670. [Patent Roll, 22 Car ii.37]

FRANCIA, SIMON, 'born beyond the seas', a grant of denization, 19 March 1688. [4 Jas ii, part 6]

FRANCIA, SIMON, in the parish of St James, Duke Place, London, 1695. [LRS.1966.112]

FRANCIS, DAVID, agent, Grange Road, Edinburgh, 1859. [ELD]

FRANCES, JACOB, in Barbados, probate 1727 PCC. [TNA]

FRANCO, ABRAHAM, an alien, was granted denization, 3 June 1699. [Patent Roll, 11 William III, pt.2.]

FRANKCOE, JACOB, a militiaman in Barbados, 1679. [TNA.CO1.44.47]

FRANCO, JACOB, in the parish of St Catherine Coleman, London, second son of **Moses Franco**, merchant in Leghorn, Italy, petitioned for a grant of coat of arms, for him and his descendants and for **Moses,**

only surviving son of his uncle **Raphael Franco** and his descendents, which was granted in 1760. [TRS.ii.166]

FRANCO, JOSEPH, in Jamaica, probate 1808, PCC. [TNA]

FRANCO, LEAH, in Jamaica, probate 1808, PCC. [TNA]

FRANK, MANSEL, a planter, resettled in Nevis, 1712. [JTP.1712.392]

FRANK, SCHLEY, born 1796 in Scotland, with **Anne Frank,** born 1796 in Scotland, **Eliza Frank,** born 1816 in Dunbartonshire, **George Frank,** born 1821 in Dunbartonshire, **James Frank,** born 1828 in Dunbartonshire, **Walter Frank,** born 1829 in Dunbartonshire, 1841. [Census]

FRANK, THOMAS, a merchant in Bristol trading with Maryland, 1773. [TNA.E190.1229.4]

FRANKEL, SIMON, born 1811 'in foreign parts', 15 College Street, Edinburgh, 1841. [Census]

FRANKEN, JACOB, a grant of denization, 4 March 1675. [Cal.SPDom. 1675.606] [Patent Roll, 27 Car ii]

FRANKLIN, BERNARD, born 1843, died 27 March 1924. [Newington MI, Edinburgh]

FRANKLIN, LAZARUS, in 1822 he was a jeweller and patent lever watch manufacturer, later a watchmaker, at 53 North Bridge, Edinburgh, his home was at 26 Gayfield Square and later at 92 Lauriston Place, Edinburgh; his wife **Miriam,** died 12 March ....., aged 39. [FJC.37][Braid Place, Edinburgh, MI]

FRANKLIN, LEWIS, born 1777 in England, a gentleman, 1 Broughton Place, Edinburgh, 1841, with **Emanuel Franklin,** born 1809 in England, a merchant. [Census]

FRANKLIN, PHINEAS, son of **Lazarus Franklin,** a jeweller, 58 North Bridge, Edinburgh, 1834. [FJC.37]

FRANKS, ABRAHAM, a widower, with his son **Abraham** and daughter **Abigail,** in the parish of St Andrew Undershaft, London, 1695. [LRS. 1966.112]

FRANKS, ANN, in the parish of All Hallows, London Wall, 1695. [LRS. 1966.112]

FRANCKS, BERNHARD, born 1796 'in foreign parts', foreign commission agent and optician, 1 Elm Row, Edinburgh, 1849, 1851, 1859. [ELD][Census][EPOD]

FRANKS, BENJAMIN, with his wife **Hester,** son **Abraham,** daughters **Abigail** and **Judith,** in the parish of All Hallows, London, 1695. [LRS. 1966.112]

FRANKS, DAVID, in Pennsylvania, a petition, 1769. [ActsPCCol.V.198]; a Loyalist claim in 1784. [TNA.AO12.42.93, etc]

FRANKS, ISAAC, died in Bath in 1736.

FRANKS, JACOB, petitioned for land on Cape Breton Island, 1769. [ActsPCCol.V.600]

FRANKS, JOHN, a servant in the parish of St Benet, Gracechurch, London, 1695. [LRS.1966.112]

FRANKS, JOHN, a victualler, with his wife **Esther,** and daughter **Elizabeth,** in the parish of St Katherine, Coleman, London, 1695. [LRS. 1966.112]

FRANKS, MICHAEL, a servant in the parish of St James, Garlickhithe, London, 1695. [LSR.1966.112]

FRANKS, MOSES, a merchant in London [?], to despatch the <u>Maria</u>, 180 tons, to New Jersey in 1756; petitioned for land on Cape Breton Island, 1769. [ActsPCCol.IV.327; V.600]

FRANKS, MOSES, jr., son of **David Franks,** settled in Philadelphia, a Loyalist in 1776, moved to Teddington, England, by 1784. [TNA.AO12.75.75/99.337/ etc]

FRANKS, NAPTHALI, charged with a breach of the peace in Hackney, London, 18 December 1738. [JH.283]

FRANKS, NAPHTALI, petitioned for land on Cape Breton Island, 1769. [ActsPCCol.V.600]

FRANSUM, JOSEPH, from Barbados aboard the bark Blessing to Providence in 1679. [TNA.CO1]

FRASSOON, RACHEL, a widow, with her bachelor son **Joseph,** in the parish of St James, Duke's Place, London, 1695. [LRS.1966.112]

FRASON, SAMUEL JOSEPH, an alien, was granted denization, 9 March 1694. [Patent Roll, 6 William and Mary, pt.1. S.P.D. Warrant book 38.496]

FREE, IZRAEL, in the parish of Christ Church, London, 1695. [LRS. 1966.112]

FREEDMAN, MORDECAI, born 1830, died 3 December 1904, his wife **Polina,** born 1843, died 2 August 1907. [Newington MI, Edinburgh]

FREEMAN, ELIAS, born 1830, died 23 September 1914, husband of **Margolith Esther,** born 1834, died 27 June 1889. [Newington MI, Edinburgh]

FREIT, AARON, 1843. [NRS.CS275.5.162]

FRIEDBERG, JULIUS, a dealer, 3 Wellington Market, Hull, 1852. [HCA]

FRIEDBERG, SOLOMON, a jeweller and silversmith, 59 Goodmangate, York, 1851. [HCA]

FUAH, MIRIAM, in the parish of St Andrew Undershaft, London, 1695. [LRS.1966.114]

FUAH, NATHAN, in the parish of St Andrew Undershaft, London, 1695. [LRS.1966.114]

FURDINANDO, NUNIS, in the parish of St Katherine Cree, London, 1695. [LRS.1966.114]

FURTADO, ISHACK ABOAB, alias **ISHAC ABOAB,** an alien, a grant of denization, 10 December 1695. [Patent Roll, 7 Wm. iii, part 4]

FURST, L., from Paris, landed at Margate in 1796, settled in Edinburgh by 1806. [FJC.5][EBR:SL115]

FURST, Reverend JACOB, born 1844, minister of the Edinburgh Jewish Congregation, died 3 November 1918, his wife **Marion** born 1850, died 4 November 1912. [Newington MI, Edinburgh]

GAAT, JOSEPH, a merchant, was admitted as a burgess of Edinburgh on 26 May 1784. [EBR]

GABAY, DAVID, a grant of denization, 2 August 1661. [Patent Roll, 2 August 1661]

GABEL, ELIAS, a German Jew, was granted a pass to travel from England to Holland, 8 November 1705. [TNA.SP44.390.330]

GABRIEL, DAVID, from Holland, landed at Gravesend, settled in Edinburgh by 1803. [EBR:SL115][FJC.5]

GABRIEL, JOHN, a vintner in Overgate, Dundee, 1837; 1840. [DD]

GALINDA, JUDITH, with her son **Abraham,** in the parish of St Katherine Cree, London, 1695. [LRS.1966.115]

GALINDO, ABRAHAM, with **Judith** his wife, in the parish of St James, Duke Place, London, 1695. [LRS.1966.115]

GARCIA, DANIEL, graduated MD from King's College, Aberdeen, on 4 February 1824, proposed by Dr John Meyer. [KCA.159]

GASPER, SAMUEL, born 1829 in Prussia, a hawker of jewelry, Nicolson Street, Edinburgh, 1851. [Census]

GAUDEN, BENJAMIN, with his wife **Elizabeth,** in the parish of All Hallows, Barking, London, 1695. [LRS.1966.117]

GEDALIA, JACOB, a German Jew, was granted a pass to travel from England to Holland, 12 June 1706. [TNA.SP44.393.6]

GEE, JOSHUA, with his wife **Sarah,** in the parish of St Matthew, Friday Street, London, 1695. [LRS.1966.117]

GEMART, ISAAC, in the parish of St Gabriel, Fenchurch, London, 1695. [LRS.1996.117]

GEMART, REBECCA, in the parish of St Gabriel, Fenchurch, London, 1695. [LRS.1996.117]

GERISH, BENJAMIN, bound from Barbados aboard the ketch Mary bound for Boston, 1678. [TNA.CO1]

GERISH, HESTER, in the parish of All Hallows, Honey Lane, London, 1695. [LRS.1966.118]

GIDEON, ROWLAND, an alien, was granted denization, 30 July 1679. [Patent Roll, 31 Car II, part 8]

GIDEON, ROWLAND, from Barbados aboard the Phoenix bound for Antigua in November 1679. [TNA.CO1]

GIDEON, ROWLAND, with his wife **Hester,** and daughter **Bara,** in the parish of All Hallows, London Wall, 1695. [LRS.1966,119]

GIDEON, SAMSON, born 1699, stockbroker, maritime insurer, and foreign currency dealer in London, died 1762.

GLASSTONE, ADELAIDE, born 1828, died 31 December 1907. [Newington MI, Edinburgh]

GOLDSTON, DAVID, born 1839, '7 years treasurer, 10 years president of the Edinburgh Hebrew Congregation', died 29 June 1911. [Newington MI, Edinburgh]

GOLDSON, THOMAS, in Port Royal, Jamaica, probate 1784 PCC. [TNA]. His will refers to his reputed son **Thomas Goldson,** his reputed daughter **Elizabeth** relict of **William Winter** a gentleman in Port Royal, his natural daughter **Ann Goldson,** his reputed son **John Goldson,** his nephew **Jeffry Knight** son of his sister **Ann Knight** in Red Lyon Square, London, his brother **William Goldson** a gentleman of Union Street, Portsmouth Common, **Aaron Nunes Henriques** a merchant in Kingston, Jamaica.

GOLLIN, BEARMAN, born 1819 in Spittalfields, London, son of Rabbi **Wolf Josephson Gollin,** a clothier in Liverpool, died 4 March 1895, husband of **Mary Marks** [1830-1906]. [Deane Road Cemetery, Liverpool]

GOLDSMIT, AARON, a decreet, 27 February 1815. [NRS.CS40.18.48]

GOMERSAL, EZEKIEL, a member of the Council of Jamaica, 1716. [JTP. 1716.14]

GOMES, ABRAHAM, grant of denization, 14 December 1694. [S.P.Dom. Warrant book 39.124]

GOMEZ, FRANCIS, a grant of denization, 9 June 1688. [Patent Roll, 4 Jas ii. 6]

GOMES, ISAACK, a militiaman in Barbados, 1679. [TNA.CO1.44.47]; with 3 children {?} in St Michael's 1680. [TNA.CO1]

GOMES, ISAAC, grant of denization, 14 December 1694. [S.P.Dom. Warrant book 39.124]

GOMES, ISAAC, a bachelor, in the parish of All Hallows, London Wall, 1695. [LRS.1966.123]

GOMEZ, MOSES, in the parish of St James, Duke's Place, London, 1695. [LRS.1966.123]

GOMMASERUS, PHINEAS, with his wife **Sarah**, and son **Jacob**, in the parish of St Katherine Cree, London, 1695. [LRS.1966,123]

GOMME-SERA, ANTHONY, a gentleman, with his wife **Rebecca**, sons **Joshua** and **Moses,** daughters **Deborah** and **Sarah,** in the parish of St Andrew Undershaft, London, 1695. [LRS.1966.123]

GONSALES, ABRAHAM COEN, a petitioner in London, 1658. [CalSPDom.Commonwealth.cxxv.58]

GONSALES, ABRAHAM, a merchant in Kingston, Jamaica, and a planter in St Ann's, 1737, [Car.3.155]; a petitioner in Jamaica, 1752. [ActsPCCol.1745-1766.151]; in Jamaica, probate 1760, PCC. [TNA]

GONSALES, EMANNUEL, born 1758, a brass founder from London, emigrated from London aboard the <u>Diana</u> bound for Maryland in 1774. [TNA,T47.9/11]

GONSALES, ISAAC, in Jamaica, probate 1764, PCC. [TNA]

GONSALES, JACOB, a merchant in Kingston, Jamaica, planter in St Ann's parish, 1737, [Car.3.155]; a petitioner in Jamaica, 1752. [ActsPCCol.1745-1766.151]; in London by 1775. [Car.3.155]

GONZALES, JACQUES, letters of denization, 16 July 1689. [CalSPDom. 1689.188]

GONSALEZ, JAMES, an alien, a grant of denization, January 1684. [Patent Roll, 34 Car ii.8]

GONSALES, MOSES ALERES COROKS JACOB, a merchant in London, executor, 1802. [Car.2.367]

GOODYER, AARON, a gentleman and a bachelor, in the parish of St Bartholemew by the Exchange, London, 1695. [LRS.1966,125]

GOSHLER, SAMUEL, a German Jew, was granted a pass to travel from England to Holland, 14 November 1705. [TNA.SP44.390.332]

GOSLER, SIMEON, a German Jew, was granted a pass to travel from England to Holland, 23 July 1706. [TNA.SP44.393.36]

GOVIA, ISAAC, a Jew in Surinam petitioned to go to Jamaica, 1676. [SPAWI.1676.818.i]

GRAZILLIER, EZECHIAL, took the Oath of Association in New York, 1696. [TNA]

GREEN, Reverend AARON LEVY, of the Central Synagogue, Bristol, 1838-1851.

GUBAY, ABRAHAM JACQUES, an alien, a grant of denization, 7 November 1667. [Patent Roll, 19 Car ii]

GUTTERES, JACOB MENDES, born in Portugal, a grant of denization, in June 1670. [Patent Roll, 22 Car ii]

GUTTUREZ, JACOB MENDEZ, merchant in Jamaica, executor of **Moses Gutturez** deceased, petition, 1739. [ActsPCCol.III.644]; in Jamaica, probate 1752, PCC. [TNA]

GUTIERES, LUDOVICUS DIOS, a grant of denization, 12 July 1661. [Patent Roll, 13 Car ii.17]

GUTIERES, MOSES, an alien, was granted denization 14 December 1694. [S.P.Dom.Warrant book.39.124]

GUTTUREZ, MOSES, deceased, his wife **Judica**, and their sons **Jacob** and **Joseph Gutturez**, daughter **Sarah** and **Leah** deceased, all in Jamaica, a petition, 1739. [ActsPCCol.III.644]

GUTIERES, RACHEL GOMES, in Jamaica, probate 1735, PCC. [TNA]

GUTTUREZ, SARAH, daughter of **Moses Gutturez** and wife of William Forbes in Jamaica, grand-daughter of **Leah Gutturez**, 1739. [ActsPCCol.III.644]

HALSE, ISAAC, and RUTH GIRDLER or HALSE, decreet of divorce, 1832. [NRS.CS46.12.162]

HAMBERG, DAVID, born 1821 in Dunbartonshire, in Kirkintilloch 1841. [Census]

HAMBURG, MOISES, a German Jew, was granted a pass to travel from England to Holland, 25 September 1706. [TNA.SP44.393.100]

HAMIAS, MOSES, in St Michael's parish, Barbados, 1679. [TNA.CO1.44.47]; with 2 children {?} in St Michael's 1680. [TNA.CO1]

HANNEMAN, MICHAEL, a jeweller and merchant of 24 Carnegie Street, Edinburgh, 1825, [FJC.6/38]; born 1786 'in foreign parts', a broker, 6 Gibbs Entry, Edinburgh, with wife **Betty Hanneman**, born 1786 'in foreign parts', 1841, [Census]; died 17 May 1861. [JBGE]

HANNEMAN, MICHAEL, died 3 July 1849. [JBGE]

HARRIS, ABRAHAM, born 1812 in Prussia, a wholesale traveller, 24 Stockwell Place, Glasgow, with his wife **Anna Harris**, born 1818 in England, and children **Hendry Harris**, born 1838 **Barnet Harris**, born 1840 in Glasgow, **Ephraim Harris**, born 1848 in Glasgow, **David Harris**, born 1850 in Glasgow, and **Rachel Harris**, born 1846 in Glasgow. [Census]

HARRIS, ABRAHAM, a militiaman in Barbados, 1679. [TNA.CO1.44.47]

HART, EPHRAIM, from Mark Lane, London, lately in New York, administration, 1840, PCC. [TNA]

HART, HYMAN, died in Bath, 1738. [BRO]

HART, ISAAC, a merchant in Newport, Rhode Island, 1765, 1769. [ActsPCCol.IV.716; V.191]

HART, JOSIAH, with his wife **Ursula,** and her son **John Wolfe,** in the parish of St Katherine Cree, London, 1695. [LRS.1966.138]

HART, NAPTHALI, a merchant in Newport, Rhode Island, 1765, 1769. [ActsPCCol.IV.716; V.191]

HART, REBECCA, daughter of **Lemon Hart** in London, married **W. J. Levi** in Barbados on 2 February 1820. [GM.90.272]

HAUSCH, NATHAN, 1748. [NRS.CS271.9713]

HAYEMS, JOSEPH, a German Jew, was granted a pass to travel from England to Holland, 25 September 1706. [TNA.SP44/393/100]

HEATH, MAHER SHAHEL HASHBETH, resettled on Nevis, 1712. [JTP. 1709-1715.383]

HECHSTETTER, JOSEPH, with his wife **Susan** in the parish of St Mary, Abchurch, London, 1695. [LRS.1966.143]

HELBERT, SAMUEL, a jeweller, with his wife **Bison,** sons **Philip, Jacob, Moses,** and **Isaack,** and daughter **Rebecca,** in the parish of St James, Duke's Place, London, 1695. [LRS.1966.144]

HENDERICH, SARAH, a German Jew, was granted a pass to travel from England to Holland, 3 January 1706. [TNA.SP44.390.362]

HENRIQUES, A. Q., born 1775, formerly in Jamaica, died in Shirley, Hampshire, on 30 May 1840. [GM.NS14.110]

HENRIQUES, AARON, was granted a pass to travel from England to Holland on 6 April 1705. [TNA.SP44.390.417]

HENRIQUES, AARON NUNES, merchant in the parish of Kingston, County Surrey, Jamaica, executor of **Thomas Goldson** late of Port Royal, Jamaica, 1785. [Car.3.226] deed appointed **Raphael Vas Da Silva** and **Isaac Isral Bernal**, merchants in London, as his attorneys in Great Britain.

HENRIQUES, ABRAHAM BUENO, an alien, born in Bayonne, was granted denization, 1 September 1669. [Patent Roll, 21 Charles II, part 2]; a militiaman in Barbados, 1679. [TNA.CO1.44.47]

HENRIQUES, ABRAHAM GOMEZ, an alien merchant, a grant of denization on 11 August 1668. [Patent Roll, 20 Car ii]

HENRIQUES, ABRAHAM, was granted a pass to travel from England to Holland on 6 April 1705. [TNA.SP44.390.417]

HENRIQUES, DANIEL BUENO, born in Spain, a merchant in Barbados, a grant of denization 24 July 1661; merchant in Barbados, petitioned to be denized, 1677. [Patent Roll, 13 Car ii][SPAWI.1661.139; 1677.556]

HENRIQUES, DAVID GOMES, 'born in foreign parts', a grant of denization' 29 June 1668. [Patent Roll, 20 Car ii]

HENRIQUES, DAVID, late of Durham, died in Newcastle, 1775, probate 11 November 1775.[TNA]

HENRIQUES, ISAAC, an alien, granted denization, 2 October 1662. [Patent Roll, 14 Car.ii.2]

HENRIQUES, ISAAC, a bachelor, in the parish of St James, Duke's Place, London, 1695. [LRS.1996.144]

HENRIQUES, JACOB BUENO, an alien, born in Bayonne, was granted denization, 1 September 1669. [Patent Roll, 21 Car II, part 2]

HENRIQUES, JACOB BUENO, junior, an alien, a grant of denization, 11 October 1687. [Patent Roll, 1 Jas ii]

HENRIQUES, JACOB, proposals, March 1768. [NRS.GD110.1328]

HENRIQUES, JACOB DE DAVID LOPES, 1712. [NRS.AC8.152]

HENRIQUES, JOSEPH BUENO, an alien, was granted denization, 9 March 1694. [Patent Roll, 6 William and Mary, pt.1. S.P.Dom. Warrant book 38.496]

HENRIQUES, JOSEPH, with his wife **Rachel,** son **Abraham,** and daughter **Esther,** in the parish of St Katharine Cree, London, 1695. [LRS.1966.144]

HENRIQUES, JOSEPH, in Jamaica, probate 1810, PCC. [TNA]

HENRIQUES, JOSHUA BUENO, an alien, born in Bayonne, was granted denization, 1 September 1669. [Patent Roll, 21 Chas II, part 2]

HENRIQUES JOSHUA BUENO, an alien, a grant of denization, 11 October 1687. [Patent Roll, 1 Jas ii]

HENRIQUES, MANUEL, an alien, a merchant in London, a grant of denization, 17 March 1687. [Patent Roll, 3 James ii, part 3]

HENRIQUES, MOSES BUENO, an alien, born in Bayonne, was granted denization, 1 September 1669. [Patent Roll, 21 Chas II, part 2]

HENRIQUES, MOSES, a merchant in Kingston, Jamaica, 1819, witness to **David Wolfe's** deed. [NRS.RD5.193.713]

HENRIQUES, PEDRO, jr., an alien, a grant of denization, 30 November 1693. [Patent Roll, 5 William and Mary 4, part 2]

HENRIQUES, PETER, the elder, an alien, a grant of denization, 17 January 1677. [Patent Roll, 28 Car ii, part3]

HENRIQUES, PETER, the younger, an alien, a grant of denization, 17 January 1677. [Patent Roll, 28 Car ii, part 3]

HENRIQUES, PETER, 'born beyond the seas', a grant of denization, 19 March 1688. [4 Jas ii, part 6]

HENRIQUES, PETER, with his wife **Sarah,** and daughter **Hesther,** in the parish of St Katherine Cree, London, 1695. [LRS.1966.144]

HENRIQUES, PETER, a gentleman, with his wife **Sarah,** son **Abraham,** and daughters **Rachel** and **Claire,** in the parish of St Gabriel, Fenchurch, London, 1695. [LRS.1966.144]

HENRIQUES, PETER, a gentleman, with his wife **Ester,** and sons **Abraham, Isaac,** and **Aron,** in the parish of St Gabriel, Fenchurch, London, 1695. [LRS.1966.144]

HENRIQUES, PIERRE, 'born beyond the seas', a grant of denization, 19 March 1688. [4 Jas ii, part 6]

HENRIQUES, RACHEL, was granted a pass to travel from England to Holland on 6 April 1705. [TNA.SP44.390.417]

HEROCH, MOSES, aged 36, born in Schadanke, Germany, a merchant from Hamburg, landed in Leith, settled in Edinburgh by 1817. [EBR:SL115][FJC.5]

HESTERMAN, ABRAHAM, in the parish of St Mary, Abchurch, London, 1695. [LRS.1966.146]

HEYMAN, ISAAC, a decreet, 1826. [NRS.CS44.95.15]

HEYMANS, JACOB, was granted a pass to travel from England to Holland on 18 April 1705. [TNA.SP44.390.433]

HIAL, JACOB, in Glasgow, 1831. [NRS.AD14.30.182]

HILLMER, JOSEPH, 1761. [NRS.AC8.1049]

HIRSCH, H.A., a merchant, 51 Reform Street, Dundee, 1853. [DD]

HIRSCHELL, SOLOMON, born 12 February 1752 in London, Chief Rabbi of Great Britain from 1802 until 1842, died 31 October 1842.

HOLLANDER, JACOB, with his wife **Hannah,** and daughter **Binah,** in the parish of St James, Duke's Place, London, 1695. [LRS.1966.152]

HOLLANDER, MOSES, in the parish of St James, Duke's Place, London, 1695. [LRS.1966.152]

HONEYMAN, DAVID, a teacher of Hebrew, St Paul's Court, house 62 Murraygate, Dundee, 1846. [DD]

HONEYMAN, MOSES, a decree, 12 April 1837. [NRS.SC39.17.4365]

HOSKINS, SIMON, with his wife **Mary,** and son **Abraham,** in the parish of St James, Duke's Place, London, 1695. [LRS.1966.155]

HOUSEN, JUDA, a Jew, was granted a pass to travel from England to Holland, 2 May 1706. [TNA.SP44.390.445]

HOUSEN, JUDE, a German Jew, was granted a pass to travel from England to Holland, 5 April 1706. [TNA.SP44.390.415a]

??HUISMAN, ABRAHAM, in New York City, probate 1748, PCC. [TNA]

HUME, MARTHA, a German Jew, was granted a pass to travel from England to Holland, 20 June 1706. [TNA.SP44.393.12]

HYEM, ABRAHAM, with his wife **Gettler,** German Jews, were granted a pass to travel from England to Holland, 1 April 1706. [TNA.SP44.390.412]

HYEMS, ESTER, a German Jew, was granted a pass to travel from England to Holland, 29 March 1706. [TNA.SP44.390.409]

HYEMS, HYEM, an articifer in Ipswich, 1796. [TJS.ii.134]

HYEMS, JACOB, a German Jew, was granted a pass to travel from England to Holland, 3 January 1706. [TNA.SP44.390.362]

HYAM, JOSEPH, son of **H.** and **Hannah Hyam** of Colchester, died 5597 aged 45. [Jewish Cemetery, St Clement's, Ipswich]

HYAM, JULIA, daughter of **Lawrence** and **Caroline Hyam** of Bury, died 30 May 5600 aged 5. [Jewish Cemetery, St Clement's, Ipswich]

HYAMS, MOSES, born 1751, a jeweller from London, bound from the port of London aboard the <u>Pennsylvania Packet</u> to Philadelphia in 1775. [TNA.T47.9/11]

HYAM, RACHEL, daughter of **Lawrence** and **Caroline Hyam** of Bury, died 19 June 5600 aged 3. [Jewish Cemetery, St Clement's, Ipswich]

HYEM, SIMON, an articifer in Ipswich, 1796. [TJS.ii.134]

HYMAN, FREIDA, born 1840, died 28 October 1913, mother of David and Reuben. [Newington MI, Edinburgh]

HYMAN, ROBERT, born 1830, died 28 November 1894, father of **Emma.** [Newington MI, Edinburgh]

HYMAN, SELRICK, born 1810, died 27 March 1883. [Newington MI, Edinburgh]

HYNDMAN, JOSEPH, a baker, 74 Vennel, Greenock. [Slater's Directory]

IMANDT, JOSEPH, teacher of modern languages, 29 Cowgate, Dundee, 1856. [DD]

INRIN, ISACK, with his wife **Ester,** in the parish of St Antholin, London, 1695. [LRS.1966.162]

ISAAC, ABRAHAM, a German Jew, was granted a pass to travel from England to Holland, 31 May 1706. [TNA.SP44.390.461]

ISAAC, ABRAHAM, a German Jew, was granted a pass to travel from England to Holland, 25 September 1706. [TNA.SP44.393.100]

ISAACS, ABRAHAM, [dead by 1758], and his wife **Hannah,** in Rhode Island, a promissory note, 1749. [ActsPCCol.iv.349]

ISAAC, ABRAHAM, a merchant in London, a bond, 9 July 1766. [OU.Rawl.msC983/69]

ISAACK, EMANUELL, a bachelor, in the parish of St James, Duke's Place, London, 1695. [LRS.1966.162]

ISAACKS, GERSON, a bachelor, in the parish of St James, Duke's Place, London, 1695. [LRS.1966.162]

ISAACS, HARTUG, a Jew, was granted a pass to travel from England to Holland, 2 May 1706. [TNA.SP44.390.445]

ISAAC, HAYEN, a German Jew, was granted a pass to travel from England to Holland, 24 June 1706. [TNA.SP44.393.14]

ISAACS, HENRY A., a decreet, 6 February 1850. [NRS.SC.Midlothian#11923]

ISAAC, HYEM, a German Jew, was granted a pass to travel from England to Holland, 23 July 1706. [TNA.SP44.393.36]

ISAACS, ISAAC, a German Jew, was granted a pass to travel from England to Holland, 5 April 1706. [TNA.SP44.390.415a]

ISAACS, J., a merchant in Liverpool, bankrupt, 1820. [SM.86.284]

ISAACKS, JACOB, a merchant in Newport, Rhode Island, 1751, 1757, 1765, a petition, 1768. [ActsPCCol.IV.143/348/717/759; V.175]

ISAACS, JACOB, sentenced to fourteen years transportation, London, November 1814. [LRS.2007.181]

ISAACS, JANE, a planter, on Nevis, 1708, [TNA.CO.152-157], resettled on Nevis, 1712. [JTP.1712.384]

ISAAC, JOHN RAPHAEL, born 1809, an engraver, lithographer and painter in Liverpool, died 1870, husband of **Sarah Amelia Coleman** [1813-1901]. [Deane Road Cemetery, Liverpool]

ISAAC, JOSEPH, born 1754, a peruke-maker, emigrated from London aboard the <u>Virginia</u> bound for Virginia, 1773. [TNAS.T47.9/11]

ISAACS, MOISES, a German Jew, was granted a pass to travel from England to Holland, 25 September 1706. [TNA.SP44.393.99]

ISAACS, MAURICE, born 1841, a Justice of the Peace and President of the Edinburgh Jewish Congregation, died 4 January 1913, his wife Melanie died 10 December 1815. [Newington MI, Edinburgh]

ISAAC, RALPH, born 1772, died 1840, husband of **Sophia ......,** born 1786, died 1867. [Deane Road Cemetery, Liverpool]

ISAACK, ROBERT, with his wife **Susan,** sons **Abraham, Henry,** daughter **Sarah,** in the parish of St Michael, Crooked Lane, London, 1695. [LRS. 1966.162]

ISAAC, SARAH, born 1825 in Edinburgh, a shop girl, Greenside Street, Edinburgh, 1841. [Census]

ISAACKSON, JACOB, a merchant, in the parish of St Katherine Coleman, London, probate 1657 PCC. [TNA]

ISLADORE, CONLAN, born 1833 in Berlin, a commercial traveller, High Street, Dundee, 1851. [Census]

ISRAEL, ABRAHAM, in the parish of St James, Duke's Place, London, 1695. [LRS.1966.162]

ISRAEL, ABRAHAM, with his wife **Sarah,** son **Jacob,** and daughter **Rebecca,** in the parish of St Andrew, Undershaft, London, 1695. [LRS. 1966.162]

ISRAL, CHARLES, a merchant, 4 Cowgate, Dundee, 1850. [DD]

ISRAEL, DAVID, in Barbados, grant of denization, 27 December 1662. [Patent Roll.14 Car.ii.7]; a militiaman in St Michael's parish, Barbados, 1679. [TNA.CO1.44.47] with 5 children {?} in St Michael's 1680. [TNA.CO1]

ISRAEL, DAVID, a German Jew, was granted a pass to travel from England to Holland, 28 June 1706. [TNA.SP44.393.18]

ISRAEL, ELIAS, a militiaman in Barbados, 1679. [TNA.CO1.44.47]

ISRAEL, HAYEN, a German Jew, was granted a pass to travel from England to Holland, 3 January 1706. [TNA.SP44.390.362]

ISRAEL, HENRY, jr., of St Ann parish, Jamaica, a petition re the condemnation of the sloop Diamond, master Joseph Rondon, 1764. a petitioner in Jamaica, 1752. [ActsPCCol.1745-1766.689]

ISRAEL, HESTER, with son Jacob, in the parish of St James, Duke's Place, London, 1695. [LRS.1966.162]

ISRAEL, ISAAC, a militiaman in Barbados, 1679. [TNA.CO1.44.47]

ISRAEL, ISRAEL, jr., in Philadelphia, probate 1812 PCC. [TNA]

ISRAEL, JACOB, a German Jew, was granted a pass to travel from England to Holland, 25 February 1706. [TNA.SP44.390.388]

ISRAEL, JOSEPH, aged 20, a planter, emigrated from London aboard the Parnassus bound for Jamaica, 1774. [TNA.T47.9/11]

ISRAEL, JUDITH, in St Michael's parish, Barbados, 1679. [TNA.CO1.44.47]; with 2 children {?} in St Michael's 1680. [TNA.CO1]

ISRAEL, MARY, a widow, with daughter Anna, in the parish of St Benet Fink, London, 1695. [LRS.1966.162]

ISRAEL, MANASSAH BEN, in London, petition, 1655. [Cal.S.P.Dom. 1655.cii.15/1; 1656.cxxv.15/20/23/58/306]

ISRAEL, PETER, aged 18, emigrated from London aboard the Parnassus bound for Jamaica, 1774. [TNA.T47.9/11]

ISRAEL, SARAH, a widow, with her daughters Rebecca, Hepsibath, and Abigail, in the parish of St Katherine, Coleman, London, 1695. [LRS. 1966.162]

ISRAEL, SHAKERLY, a planter, resettled on Nevis, 1712. [JTP.1712.386]

ISRAEL, SHAKERLY and CATHERINE, resettled on Nevis, 1712. [JTP. 1709-1715.386]

ISRAEL, SOLOMON, on Nevis 1678, [TNA.CO1]; on Nevis 1708, [TNA.CO152-157]; resettled on Nevis, 1712. [JTP.1709-1715.386]; witness to the will of Azariah Pinney on Nevis, 1718. [TNA]

ISRAEL, WILLIAM, aged 17, emigrated from London aboard the Parnassus bound for Jamaica, 1774. [TNA.T47.9/11]

ISRAEL, versus DONALDSON, an appeal from Jamaica, 1765. [ActsPCCol.1765.667]

ITALIANO, SIMON, with his wife Hester, and daughter Rebecca, in the parish of St James, Duke's Place, London, 1695. [LRS.1966.163]

JACHMANN, JOHN BENJAMIN, from Belarus{?} ['Borsssus'], graduated MD from Edinburgh University, 1789. [EMG.21]

JACKSON, ABRAHAM, born 1785, died 1839. [Deane Road Cemetery, Liverpool]

JACKSON, DAVID, born 1780, draper, died 1854, [TNA.Prob.11/2194]; husband of Katherine Ralph, born 1780, died 1839. [Deane Road Cemetery, Liverpool]

JACOBS, A., a watchmaker and jeweller, Edinburgh, 1832.

JACOBS, AARON, born 1771 in Prussia, a broker, 3 Renfrew Street, Glasgow, with daughter Amelia Jacobs or Philipsboreu, and grandson Jacob Philipsboreu, 1851. [Census]

JACOBS, AARON, a jeweller in Manor Alley, Hull, 1790.[HCA]

JACOBS, AARON, a spirit dealer in Potter Row, Edinburgh, 1810, at 21 College Street, Edinburgh, 1812, a jeweller and watchmaker, 338 Cowgate, Edinburgh, with home at 391 Lawnmarket, Edinburgh, 1820, in 1824 at 31 North Richmond Street, Edinburgh, and in 1832 at 41 North Richmond Street, [FJC.38]

JACOBS, AARON, partner in the firm **R. Jacobs** and Company, hatters in Edinburgh, decreets, 1824-1825. [NRS.CS44.50.50; CS44.91.96; CS44.104.12]

JACOB, ABRAHAM, merchant in London, trading with Virginia and Bermuda, 1619.[ActsPCCol.I.27]; gentleman of HM wine cellar, 1624. [NRS.NRAS.332.M9.14]; customs farmer of London, 1626. [APCE. 1626.101/102/152/153/319]

JACOB, ABRAHAM, a merchant's agent in London or Madeira, 1681. [LRS.2002.236]

JACOB, ALEXANDER, with his wife **Elizabeth,** sons **Alexander** and **Barnett,** in the parish of St Mary, Aldermanbury, London, 1695. [LRS. 1966.164]

JACOBS, BENEDICK, a German Jew, was granted a pass to travel from England to Holland, 25 September 1706. [TNA.SP44.393.99]

JACOBS, Reverend BENJAMIN, in Hull, 1852. [HCA.C.DJC.2.1.12.4]

JACOBS, BETHEL, in Hull, 1852. [HCA.C.DJC.2.1.12.4]

JACOBS, DANIEL, with **Jude** and **Rebecca Jacobs,** German Jews, were granted a pass to travel from England to Holland, 28 June 1706. [TNA.SP44.393.18]

JACOBS, DAVID, with his wife **Rose,** daughters **Eve, Sarah, Judith, Frummutt,** and son **Mordecai,** in the parish of St James, Duke's Place, London, 1695. [LRS.1966.164]

JACOBS, DAVID, a poor Jew, was granted a pass to travel from England to Holland, 10 October 1706. [TNA.SP44.393.172]

JACOBS, ELIZABETH, a lease in Bristol, 1739. [BRO.1342.269.10]

JACOB, EMANUEL, a servant, in the parish of St John Zachary, London, 1695. [LRS.1966.164]

JACOBS, EMANUEL, a German Jew, was granted a pass to travel from England to Holland, 13 June 1706. [TNA.SP44.393.7]

JACOBS, FRUME, aged 15, born in Amsterdam, residing in Canongate, Edinburgh, by 1803. [EBR.SL115]

JACOBS, GETTLECK, a German Jew, was granted a pass to travel from England to Holland, 25 September 1706. [TNA.SP44.393.99]

JACOBS, ISAAC, of Amsterdam, was granted a pass to travel from England to Holland on 4 March 1706. [TNA.SP44.390.392]

JACOBS, ISAAC, a German Jew, was granted a pass to travel from England to Holland, 18 September 1706. [TNA.SP44.393.89]

JACOBS, ISAAC, in Bristol, 1793. [Bristol Directory, 1793/1794]

JACOB, ISRAEL, of the Parade Row Synagogue, Hull, 1826. [HCA.C.DJC]

JACOBS, J., a glass manufacturer in Bristol, a bankrupt, 1820. [SM. 86.284]

JACOBS, JACOB, was granted a pass to go to the Low Countries for two years in 1626. [APCE.1626.4]

JACOB, JOHN, eldest son of Abraham Jacob a customs farmer of London, 1626. [APCE.1626,153]

JACOBS, JONAS, a German Jew, was granted a pass to travel from England to Holland, 11 September 1706. [TNA.SP44.393.85]

JACOBS, JOSEPH, with his wife **Cyrilia,** sons **Jacob** and **Nathan,** in the parish of St James, Duke's Place, London, 1695. [LRS.1966.164]

JACOBS, JOSEPH, with his wife **Frummutt,** sons **Jonathan, Isaack,** and daughter **Binah,** in the parish of St James, Duke's Place, London, 1695. [LRS.1966.164]

JACOBS, JOSEPH, a poor Jew, was granted a pass to travel from England to Holland, 10 October 1706. [TNA.SP44.393.172]

JACOBS, JOSEPH, a poor Jew, was granted a pass to travel from England to Holland, 8 November 1706. [TNA.SP44.393.187]

JACOB, JOSEPH, probate Bristol 1744.

JACOBS, JOSEPH, probate Bristol 1791.

JACOBS, JOSEPH, born 1826 in England, a clothier's assistant, 6 Miller Street, Glasgow, 1851. [Census]

JACOBS, JUDAH, aged 46, died in St Kitts on 5 July 1825. [Car.1.134]

JACOBS, LUCAS, a merchant stranger in London, factor for **Jurien Hennell, Wolfet Willems** and Company merchants and citizens of Danzig, **Peter Michiel** and **Remholt Eggerdens** citizens and aldermen of Koenigberg in Prussia, a petitioner 29 June 1626. [APCE.1626.39]

JACOBS, MANUEL, was granted a pass to travel from England to Holland on 6 April 1705. [TNA.SP44.390.417]

JACOBS, MOSES, born 1751, a jeweller from London, bound from the port of London aboard the <u>Pennsylvania Packet</u> to Philadelphia in 1775. [TNA.T47.9/11]

JACOB, MOSES, broker, 32 George IV Bridge, Edinburgh, 1858, 1859, [EPOD][ELD]; died 11 May 1865, inventory, Commissariat of Edinburgh. [NRS]

JACOBS, NATA, a German Jew, was granted a pass to travel from England to Holland, 24 May 1706. [TNA.SP44.390.458]

JACOBS, NATHAN, a German Jew, was granted a pass to travel from England to Holland, 17 June 1706. [TNA.SP44.393.9]

JACOBS, NOAH, a German Jew, was granted a pass to travel from England to Holland, 18 June 1706. [TNA.SP44.393.10]

JACOBS, PICKENS, born 'in foreign parts' 1781, a tailor, 10 North Richmond Street, Edinburgh, 1841. [Census]

JACOBS, REBECCA, a German Jew, was granted a pass to travel from England to Holland, 23 September 1706. [TNA.SP44.393.96]

JACOBS, R., a hat manufacturer, at 2 Katherine Street, Edinburgh, 1824, and by 1826 he was at 131 High Street, Edinburgh. [FJC.38]; a sederunt book, 1825-1826. [NRS.CS96.3676]

JACOBS, or APPERLEY, ROSA, born 1820 in England, a visitor at 10 Battery Place, Rothesay, Bute, Scotland, 1851. [Census]

JACOB, SAMUEL, a merchant in Bristol, 1696. [TNA.E190.1152/3]

JACOB, SAMUEL, aged 20, a tailor from Westminster, an indentured servant bound from London to Maryland aboard the Speedwell in 1772. [TNA.T47.9/11]

JACOB, SAWKIN, born 1811 in Prussia or Poland, a broker, Nicolson Street, Edinburgh, 1851. [Census]

JACOBS, SIMON, a servant, in the parish of St Edmund, Lombard Street, London, 1695. [LRS.1966.164]

JACOBS, TRUMIE, from Amsterdam, landed at Gravesend, settled in Edinburgh by 1803. [EBR:SL115][FJC.5]

JACOBS, WOLF, a German Jew, was granted a pass to travel from England to Holland, 14 November 1705. [TNA.SP44.390.332]

JACOBSON, ANN, in the parish of All Hallows the Great, London, 1695. [LRS.1966.164]

JACOBSON, HANNAH, in the parish of St Margaret Pattens, London, 1695. [LRS.1966.164]

JACOBSON, HENRY, a bachelor aged 24, in the parish of All Hallows the Great, London, 1695. [LRS.1966.164]

JACOBSEN, ISAAC, a merchant in Holland, 1657. [NRS.AC2.1]

JACOBSON, JACOB, born 1679, in the parish of All Hallows the Great, London, 1695. [LRS.1966.164]

JACOBSON, SOLOMON, was granted a passport to travel from Hull to Hamburg, 17 February 1800. [HCA.C.BRE.7.3.18]

JACOBSON, THEODORE, a bachelor, in the parish of All Hallows the Great, London, 1695. [LRS.1966.164]

JAGO, MOSES HAMOS, an alien residing in Barbados, a grant of denization 20 February 1663. [Patent Roll, 15 Car ii]

JAKABOUSKI, ..., teacher of foreign languages, at Mrs Pearson's, 9 South Tay Street, Dundee, 1840. [DD]

JAFFE, ..., a line and yarn merchant, 29 Cowgate, Dundee, 1850, 1853; merchants, 50 St Andrews Street, Dundee, 1856. [DD]

JARMAN, MOSES, a bachelor, in the parish of St Gregory by St Paul's, London, 1695. [LRS.1966.165]

JEWSON, ABEL, a decreet, 12 December 1825. [NRS.SC.Midlothian#10671]

JEWSON, SOLOMON, professor of music, 44 South Bridge, Edinburgh, 1858. [EPOD]

JEZEROON, SARAH, with her son **Isaack,** in the parish of St James, Duke's Place, London, 1695. [LRS.1966.167]

JOACHIM, JOSEPH, a German Jew, was granted a pass to travel from England to Holland, 25 February 1706. [TNA.SP44.390.388]

JOADE, SARAH, in the parish of St Lawrence Jewry, London, 1695. [LRS.1966.167]

JOEL, HENRY, born 1829, son of late Reverend **Moss Joel,** died 3 December 1908. [Newington MI, Edinburgh]

JOEL, MOSES, from London to Edinburgh in 1816; reader at the synagogue, 19 North Richmond Street, Edinburgh, 1835; 18 Drummond Street, Edinburgh, 1857. [EPOD]; a decreet, 8 November 1842. [NRS.SC.Midlothian#7824][FJC.20]

JOLIFFE, JOSEPH, born 1819 in England, a painter and paperhanger in West Dock Street, Dundee, 1841, [Census]; a japanner, 21 Union Street, Dundee, 1853,1856; house Lindsay Street, Dundee, 1853. [DD]

JONAS, NAHEMIA, a Jew, was granted a pass to travel from England to Holland, 2 May 1706. [TNA.SP44.390.445]

JONAS, REBECCA, born 1832, wife of **Isaac Jonas,** died 1857. [Betholom MI, Birmingham]

JONATHAN, DAVID, a German Jew, was granted a pass to travel from England to Holland, 4 September 1706. [TNA.SP44.393.78]

JONATHAN, HENDRY, a German Jew, was granted a pass to travel from England to Holland, 6 August 1706. [TNA.SP44.393.51]

JONG, SALOMON, a German Jew, was granted a pass to travel from England to Holland, 11 April 1706. [TNA.SP44.390.422]

JOOS, ANNA, born 1827 in Germany, a nurse, 11 Somerset Place, Glasgow, 1851. [Census]

JOSEPH, AARON, 1819, reference in David Wolfe's deed. [NRS.RD5.193.713]

JOSEPH, BENJAMIN, a widower, an assessor, with son Benjamin, daughters Elizabeth, Sarah, and Mary, in the parish of St Michael's, Crooked Lane, London, 1595. [LRS.1966.170]

JOSEPH, DAVID, a German Jew, was granted a pass to travel from England to Holland, 30 April 1706. [TNA.SP44.390.443]

JOSEPH, JOHN, with his wife Rebecca, son John, and daughter Rachel, in the parish of St Margaret, New Fish Street, London, 1695. [LRS.1966.170]

JOSEPH, NATHAN SOLOMON, born 1834, a social reformer and philanthropist, died 1909.

JOSEPH, SAMUEL, from Plymouth, Devon, settled in Philadelphia, Pennsylvania, later in Cincinatti, Ohio, probate 1827, PCC, relict Rebecca Joseph. [TNA]

JOSLIN, DANIEL, with his wife Rebecca, in the parish of All Hallows, London Wall, 1695. [LRS.1966.170]

JOZEZ, FRANCIS, a merchant, was admitted as a burgess and guilds-brother of Edinburgh on 9 October 1845. [EBR]

JUDA, ABRAHAM, a German Jew, was granted a pass to travel from England to Holland, 2 August 1706. [TNA.SP44.393.46]

JUDAH, ABRAHAM, trading with McNeil, Sadler, & Claxton in St Kitts, 1759. [NRS.CS96.4370]

JUDA, ISAAC, a German Jew, was granted a pass to travel from England to Holland, 18 September 1706. [TNA.SP44.393.89]

JUDA, JONATHAN, a German Jew, was granted a pass to travel from England to Holland, 7 February 1706. [TNA.SP44.390.376]

JUDA, SARAH, a German Jew, was granted a pass to travel from England to Holland, 18 September 1706. [TNA.SP44.393.89]

JUITT, ANTONY, with his wife **Rachel,** and daughter **Elizabeth,** in the parish of St Martin Vintry, London, 1695. [LRS.1966.170]

JULIUS, HARRIS, born 1850, died 12 May 1913.[Newington MI, Edinburgh]

JURDEN, ABRAHAM, with his wife **Susan,** and daughter **Sarah,** in the parish of St Michael, Pasternoster Royal, London, 1695. [LRS.1966.170]

KASNER, BARNET, in San Francisco, California, son of **Isaac Kasner,** administration, 1851, PCC. [TNA]

KAUFMAN, SOPHIA, born 1842, wife of **Morris** ....., died 23 February 1897. [Newington MI, Edinburgh]

KEASON, ISAAC, a servant, in the parish of St Gabriel, Fenchurch, London, 1695. [LRS.1966.171]

KEMM, BENJAMIN, a bachelor, in the parish of St Benet, Sherehog, London, 1695. [LRS.1966.171]

KHONE, JACOB and JOHN, petition, 1777. [NRS.CS233.K2.1]

KHUHFF & MEYER, bankers in London, letter, 5 January 1771; receipt, 12 September 1771. [NRS.NRAS.2177.bundle 5048; 332.C3.1111]

KINDERMAN, MICHAEL, with his wife **Sarah,** in the parish of St Michael, Pater Noster Royal, London, 1695. [LRS.1966.174]

KING, ABRAHAM, an apprentice, in the parish of All Hallows, Barking, London, 1695. [LRS.1695.174]

KING, BENJAMIN, a bachelor, in the parish of St Alphage, London, 1695. [LRS.1966.174]

KING, HEZEKIAH, an assessor, with his wife **Esther,** in the parish of St Clement, Eastcheap, London, 1695. [LRS.1966.174]

KING, MERIAM, a widow, with her daughter **Meriam,** in the parish of Christ Church, London, 1695. [LRS.1966.174]

KING, MOSES, in the parish of St Katherine Cree, London, 1695. [LRS.1695.174]

KISHMAN, MARGARET, born 1819 in Falkirk, a staymaker, 46 St Leonard Street, Edinburgh, 1851. [Census]

???KISSAM, BENJAMIN, from America, graduated MD from Edinburgh University, 1784. [EMG.17]

KLAR, R., born 1847, died 18 February 1912. [Piershill MI, Edinburgh]

KRONHEIM, JOSEPH M., born 1811 'in foreign parts', a master engraver, 6 Mansfield Place, Edinburgh, 1841. [Census]

LABATTO, ABRAHAM COHEN, a grant of denization, 2 August 1661. [Patent Roll, 13 Car ii]

LACON, JOSEPH, a German Jew, was granted a pass to travel from England to Holland, 25 September 1706. [TNA.SP44.393.100]

LAGUNA, DANIEL ISRAEL LOPEZ, born in France around 1660, a Marrano, moved to Spain, later Jamaica, then London. [TJS.iii.46]

LOGONA, LOPER DAVID, probate Jamaica, 1735. [BM.Add MS 21,931]

LAGUNA, LOPEZ CLARON, probate Jamaica, 1743. [BM.Add MS 21,931]

LAMEGO, AARON, in Jamaica, probate 1747, PCC. [TNA]

LAMEGO, AARON, in Jamaica, probate 1807, PCC. [TNA]

LAMEGO, ESTER, in Jamaica, probate 1767, PCC. [TNA]

LEMEGO, ISAAC, a petitioner in Jamaica 1752; formerly a merchant in Jamaica, later in Stoke Newington, Middlesex, father of **Sarah Lopes**

wife of **Jacob Torres**, also of **Abigail Baruh Lousada**, and **Rebecca Mendes Da Costa**, [ActsPCCol.1745-1766.151][Car.2.367]; probate 1767, PCC. [TNA][Car.3.155]

LAMERA, AARON, executor of **Jacob De Castro**, a petitioner in Jamaica, 1752. [ActsPCCol.1745-1766.151]

LANZADE, AARON BARUCH, a merchant in Barbados, a petition, 1681. [SPAWI.1681.198]

LARA, BENJAMIN, graduated MD from Aberdeen University 1814, later a Fellow of the Royal College of Physicians. [NRS.NRAS.726.3.245]

LASERS, HERTOG, a German Jew, was granted a pass to travel from England to Holland, 11 February 1706. [TNA.SP44.390.379]

LASERS, SAMUEL, a German Jew, was granted a pass to travel from England to Holland, 11 February 1706. [TNA.SP44.390.379]

LAURIER, ALFRED, aged 10 months, died 1836. [Braid Place MI, Edinburgh]

LAURIER, ARTHUR, aged ... months, died 1833. [Braid Place MI, Edinburgh]

LAZAR, JOHN, born 1 December 1801 in Edinburgh, married in London on 2 November 1825, emigrated aboard the Lady MacNaughton bound for Sydney, New South Wales, in 1836, moved to New Zealand in 1763, he died on 7 June 1879. He was father of **Abraham**, **Samuel**, **Rachel**, **Victoria**, and others. [OSJ.16]

LAZARUS, BENJAMIN, born 1814 in England, a clothier's manager, 6 Miller Street, Glasgow, with **Rebecca Lazarus**, born 1819 in England, a housekeeper, 1851. [Census]

LAZARUS, SAMUEL, a German Jew, was granted a pass to travel from England to Holland, 22 November 1705. [TNA.SP44.390.336]

LEAPER, ISRAEL, master of the Pearl, 1718. [NRS.GD158.1685]

LEATAD, MORDECAY, a German Jew, was granted a pass to travel from England to Holland, 24 June 1706. [TNA.SP44.393.14]

LEBBENNAN, SAMUEL, born 1803 in Poland, an oil cloth manufacturer, 109 North Hanover Street, Glasgow, wife **Rachel,** born in Poland 1803, sons **Jacob,** born 1828 in Poland, and **Abraham,** born1841 in Glasgow, daughters **Mary** born 1834 in Poland, and **Betsy,** born 1837 in Poland, 1851. [Census]

LEEFFS, ISAAC, an apprentice, in the parish of St Michael, Bassishaw, London, 1695. [LRS.1966.182]

LEMON, MOSES, a surgeon, married **Maria Solomon,** daughter of **Dr Solomon,** Gilead House, Liverpool, on 1 February 1815. [SM.77.293]

LETUZEY, ISAAC, a bachelor, in the parish of St Benet Fink, London, 1695. [LRS.1966.184]

LEVENSON, JAMES, born 1789 'in foreign parts', a sealing wax manufacturer in Glasgow, with **Benjamin,** born in England 1821, **Lewis** born 1826 in Lanarkshire, **Daniel** born 1828 in Lanarkshire, **Elizabeth** born 1833 in Lanarkshire, **Sarrah** born 1835 in Lanarkshire, 1841. [Census]

LEVENSTON, MICHAEL JACOB, with his sons **Solomon Alexander, Samuel, William,** and **Joseph,** medical herbalists, from Edinburgh to Glasgow in 1850. [SCJ.24]

LEVENSTON, JOSEPH, a medical herbalist, father of **Soloman Levenston** born 1858 in Aberdeen. [CJ.19]

LEVI, ABRAHAM, was granted a pass to travel from England to Holland, 30 July 1705. [TNA.SP44.393.43]

LEVI, ABRAHAM, a poor Jew, was granted a pass to travel from England to Holland, 10 October 1706. [TNA.SP44.393.172]

LEVI, DAVID, a German Jew, was granted a pass to travel from England to Holland, 4 July 1706. [TNA.SP44.393.23]

LEVI, DAVID, born 1742 in London, a scholar, died in 1801. [GM.71.934]

LEVI, ELIZABETH REBECCA, daughter of **Moses Levi** of Ipswich, died 20 May 5609. [Jewish Cemetery, St Clement's, Ipswich]

LEVI, I., a glass grinder and flowerer, Closegate, Newcastle, 1778. [Newcastle Directory]

LEVI, JONATHAN, a German Jew, was granted a pass to travel from England to Holland, 5 August 1706. [TNA.SP44.393.46]

LEVI, J., & Co., chemical apparatus makers and glass blowers, 104 High Street, Edinburgh, 1820. [CDS]

LEVI, JOSEPH, a German Jew, was granted a pass to travel from England to Holland, 24 May 1706. [TNA.SP44.390.458]

LEVI, JOSEPH, a German Jew, was granted a pass to travel from England to Holland, 17 June 1706. [TNA.SP44.393.9]

LEVI, JOSEPH, an articifer in Ipswich, 1796. [TJS.ii.134]

LEVI, JOSEPH, a quill-maker in Glasgow, at 2 Salisbury Street, Edinburgh, in 1826, died of cholera 12 September 1832, first person to be buried in Glasgow Necropolis. [FJC.39]

LEVI, LAZARUS, an articifer in Ipswich, 1796. [TJS.ii.134]

LEVI, MOSES, aged 25, a poulterer from Paddington, and his wife **Hester Levi** aged 18, emigrated from London aboard the Princess Carolina bound for Jamaica in 1774. [TNA.T47.9/11]

LEVI, PHILIP, a German Jew, was granted a pass to travel from England to Holland, 5 August 1706. [TNA.SP44.393.46]

LEVI, PHILIP, 1829. [NRS.CS271.60850]

LEVI, SAMUEL, a German Jew, was granted a pass to travel from England to Holland, 21 June 1706. [TNA.SP44.393.13]

LEVI, SAMUEL, an articifer in Colchester, Essex, 1796. [TJS.ii.134]

LEVI, SIMON, with his wife **Rachel,** and son **Isaac,** in the parish of St Katherine Cree, London, 1695. [LRS.1966.184]

LEVI, SIMON, 1823. [NRS.CS271.47812]

LEVI, SIMPSON, charged with a breach of the peace in Hackney, London, 18 December 1738. [JH.283]

LEVI, SOLON, a German Jew, was granted a pass to travel from England to Holland, 3 January 1706. [TNA.SP44.390.363]

LEVI, W. J., from Barbados, married **Rebecca**, daughter of **Levian Hart** in London on 2 February 1820. [GM.90.272]

LEVIAN, MOSES, in Hamburg, Germany, and his wife **Elizabeth**, 1819, reference to in **David Wolfe's** deed. [NRS.RD5.193.713]

LEVIN, GUMFRIG, from Gothenburg, landed at Bo'ness, settled in Edinburgh by 1806. [FJC.5][EBR:SL115]

LEVIS, ABRAHAM, a hairdresser in Blanket Row, Hull, 1791

LEVITT, JOHN, from London, a merchant in Edinburgh, 1823. [NRS.CS44/1823]

LEVY, ABRAHAM, aged 35, born abroad, a traveller, 2 Pipewellgate, North Side, Gateshead, 1841. [Census]

LEVY, ABRAHAM, a decree, 1 December 1847. [NRS.SC39.10812]

LEVY, ARABELLA, a lease in College Green, Bristol, lease, 1845. [BRO. 785.23]

LEVY, ASHUR, in Gower Street, Bedford Square, London, formerly in New York City, probate 1846 PCC. [TNA]

LEVY, AUGUSTUS SAMUEL, born 1815, a fruit merchant in Liverpool, died 1888, husband of **Miriam Tobias,** born 1815, died 1895. [Deane Road Cemetery, Liverpool]

LEVY, BARRU, with his wife **Eve,** in the parish of St James, Duke's Place, London, 1695. [LRS.1966.184]

LEVY, BENJAMIN, 'born beyond the seas', a grant of denization, 19 March 1688. [4 Jas ii, part 6]

LEVY, BENJAMIN, with his wife **Frawcha,** in the parish of St James, Duke's Place, London, 1695. [LRS.1966.184]

LEVY, BENJAMIN, a merchant, with his wife **Isabell,** sons **Michael, Moses,** and daughter **Abigail,** in the parish of St Katherine, Coleman, London, 1695. [LRS.1966.184]

LEVY, CLARA, a servant, in the parish of St Katherine, Coleman, London, 1695. [LRS.1966.184]

LEVY, DAVID, in Hull, 1851. [HCA.C.DJC.4.2]

LEVY, ELEAZER, a merchant in Quebec, a petition, 1768. [ActsPCCol.V. 142/143]

LEVY, H. & J., opticians in Bristol, 1793. [Bristol Directory, 1793/1794]

LEVY, HANNAH, in the parish of All Hallows, London Wall, 1695. [LRS. 1966.184]

LEVY, Mrs HANNAH, died 6 February 1847, aged 48. [JBGE]

LEVY, HENRY, born 15 January 1816, died 10 February 1877. [Newington MI, Edinburgh]

LEVY, HENRY, decree, Midlothian, 1851. [NRS.SC39.12521]

LEVY, ISAAC, with his wife Rose, and son Borrow, in the parish of St Katherine, Coleman, London, 1695. [LRS.1966.184]

LEVY, ISAACK, with his wife Gallibale, daughters Sarah, Rachel, and son Isaack, in the parish of St James, Duke's Place, London, 1695. [LRS.1966.184]

LEVY, ISAACK, with his wife Ellenore, and sons Moses, Michael, in the parish of St James, Duke's Place, London, 1695. [LRS.1966.184]

LEVY, ISAAC, in America, 1755. [Car.1.254]

LEVY, ISAAC, formerly of Broad Street, London, later resident in Philadelphia, a petition re lands in Georgia, 1755, a petitioner in Jamaica, 1752. [ActsPCCol.1745-1766.316]

LEVY, ISAAC, in Church Lane, Hull, 1766. [HCA.C.DJC]

LEVY, ISAAC, of Lancaster Court, London, a petition re lands in Georgia, 1767. [ActsPCCol.V.114/115]

LEVY, ISAAC, petition for land on Cape Breton Island, 1769. [ActsPCCol.V.600]

LEVY, ISAAC, born 1816 'in foreign parts', a merchant, 29 College Street, Glasgow. 1841. [Census]

LEVY, J., glass-dealer, Hemming's Row, London, bankrupt, 1825. [SM. 95.509]

LEVY, JACOB, of Harwich, died 6 August 1829 aged 57. [Jewish Cemetery, St Clement's, Ipswich]

LEVY, JACOB, a watchmaker and jeweller, 7 Overgate, Dundee, 1855. [DD]

LEVY, JOHN, a watchmaker and jeweller, Overgate, Dundee, 1856.[DD]

LEVY, JOSEPH, with his wife **Hannah,** and son **Isaack,** in the parish of St James, Duke's Place, London, 1695. [LRS.1966.184]

LEVY, JOSEPH, a furrier at 37 Hanover Street, Edinburgh, 1834. [FJC. 38]

LEVY, MICHAEL, with his wife **Leah,** sons **Mordecai, Isaack,** and daughters **Judith, Leah,** in the parish of St James, Duke's Place, London, 1695. [LRS.1966.184]

LEVY, MICHAEL, a merchant and a bachelor, in the parish of St Katherine, Coleman, London, 1695. [LRS.1966.184]

LEVY, MICHAEL, born 1765, from Kingston, Jamaica, died in London on 12 April 1845. [GM.NS23.671]

LEVY, MICHAEL, a watchmaker in Hull, 1770. [HCA]

LEVY, MICHAEL ABRAHAM, decrees, 7 October 1846; 25 March 1847. [NRS.SC39.10086/10340]; tailor, clothier and outfitter, 26 Union Street, Aberdeen, 1849, [Aberdeen Directory]; a clothier, hatter, and hosier, 24 Reform Street, Dundee, 1850; clothier and outfitter, 73-74 High Street, Dundee, house in Edinburgh, 1856. [DD]; clothier and woollen draper, 94/96/98 South Bridge, Edinburgh, and 1 Tolbooth Wynd, Leith; house 21 Clarendon Crescent, 1859. [ELD]; merchant in Edinburgh, sasines etc., 1850s. [NAS.RS27.66.82/222, 68.277, 69.83, 77.210]; a merchant in Brussels, deeds, 1864. [NAS.RS27.85.136/157]; husband of **Hannah Ashenheim.** [FJC.38]

LEVY, MORDECAY, a poor Jew, was granted a pass to travel from England to Holland, 31 October 1706. [TNA.SP44.393.185]

LEVY, MORRIS, son of **Lazarus Levy** of London, died 8 January 5610 aged 42. [Jewish Cemetery, St Clement's, Ipswich]

LEVY, MOSES, took the Oath of Association in New York, 1696. [TNA]

LEVY, MOSES, a merchant in New York, 1720. [LMD]

LEVI, MOSES, born 1749, a poulterer from Paddington, London, with his wife **Hester Levi**, born 1756, emigrated from London aboard the Princess Carolina bound for Jamaica in 1774. [TNA.T47.9/11]

LEVY, P., furrier to His Majesty, Hurcheson Street, Glasgow, 1817. [Glasgow Chronicle, 28 January 1817][SCJ.18]

LEVY, PHILIP, a furrier 56 Bridge Street, Edinburgh, 1820, [CDS]; a merchant in Edinburgh, 1825, [FJC.6/32];a furrier in Edinburgh, trust deed 1829, [NRS.CS44.1828, Levy]; furrier to His Majesty, 52 Princes Street, Edinburgh, house 60 Princes Street, 1835. [EPOD]; interim factor, 1840. [NRS.SC.39#5785]; a decreet, 1 September 1853. [NRS.SC.39# 13105]; fur merchant, 33 George Street, Edinburgh, 1859. [ELD]; died 21 July 1862, inventory 1862, Commissariat of Edinburgh. [NRS] **Hannah Levy**, his wife, died aged 47 in 1847.

LEVY, RACHEL, in the parish of St James, Duke's Place, London, 1695. [LRS.1966.184]

LEVY, RACHEL, a decree, 27 August 1852. [NRS.SC39.12792]

LEVY, or RUSSEL, ROSETTA, relict of **Wolfe Levy** a furrier, died 25 August 1857, inventory, Commissary of Lanark, 1857, [NRS]

LEVY, SAMUEL, a widower, in the parish of St James, Duke's Place, London, 1695. [LRS.1966.184]

LEVY, SARAH, a servant, in the parish of St Katharine, Coleman, London, 1695. [LRS.1966.184]

LEVY, SOLOMON, 'born beyond the seas', a grant of denization, 19 March 1688. [4 Jas ii, part 6]

LEVY, SOLOMON, leases in Bristol, 1840. [BRO.785.17-20; 5074.1]

LEVY, THOMAS, partner of Richard Dobson in Liverpool, died in St Pierre, Martinique, on 6 October 1794. [GM.64.1150]

LEVY, WOOLF, born 1781 'in foreign parts', a furrier and merchant in Glasgow, with **Rosetta Levy,** born 1791 'in foreign parts',1841. [Census]; a skinner, was admitted as a burgess of Glasgow on 22 November 1823. [GBR]; residing in Argyll Street, Glasgow, 1843. [SCJ. 22]

LEVYS, HENRIETTA, born 1772, widow of **Philip Levys** in Jamaica, died in Notting Hill, London, 11 September 1852. [GM.NS38.439]

LEW, THAMER, a servant, in the parish of St Lawrence, Pountney, London, 1695. [LRS.1966.184]

LEWISOHN, GUMPERTZ, graduated MD from ...... College, Aberdeen, 1775. [CJ]

LEWIN, RACHEL, a German Jew, was granted a pass to travel from England to Holland, 18 May 1706. [TNA.SP44.390.453]

LEWIS, GEORGE, goldsmith, Mosley Street, Newcastle, 1823. [Newcastle Directory]

LEWIS, NATHAN, 1829. [NRS.CS271.48764]

LEWIS, REBECCA, probate Jamaica, 1735. [BM. Add. MS.21,931]

LEWISOHN, GUMPERTZ, graduated MD in Aberdeen, 1775. [CJ]

LIEBE, JACOB DETTOVE, decreet, 1813. [NRS.CS38.8.82]

LIEBMAN & LAZARUS, silversmiths in Bristol, 1793. [Bristol Directory, 1793/1794]

LINDO, ESTHER, daughter of **Alexander Lindo,** married **A. M. Belisario,** in Kingston, Jamaica, in 1791. [GM.61.774]

LINDEY, MEYER HENRY, born 1850, died 20 October 1903. [Newington MI, Edinburgh]

LINDOW, ISAAC, with his wife **Leah,** and daughters **Judith, Rachel, Constance,** in the parish of St Andrew Undershaft, London, 1695. [LRS. 1966.186]

LINFERD, BENJAMIN, with his wife **Sarah,** in the parish of St Alphage, London, 1695. [LRS.1966.186]

LIPDRY, JACOB, aged 30, a baker from London, an indentured servant aboard the Speedwell bound from London to Maryland in 1772. [TNA.T47.9/11]

LIPITZ, SOLOMON ZALMEN, born 1809, died 21 August 1909. [Piershill MI, Edinburgh]

LIPMAN, HENRY, born 1801 in England, a pencil and quill dresser, 9 Greenside Place, Edinburgh, 1830-1835, a quill manufacturer in Glasgow, 1841; died 29 June 1858. [FJC.39][Census][Braid Place MI, Edinburgh]

LIPMAN, JAMES, born 1808 in Hamburg, a commission agent and linen merchant, 15 Cowgate, Dundee, house 8 Westfield Place, Perth Road, Dundee, wife **Ida** born 1825 in Hamburg, daughter **Cecilia** born 1849 in Dundee, daughter **Bertha** born 1851 in Dundee;1850; 1851;1856. [DD] [Census]

LIPMAN, JOHN, a black lead and pencil manufacturer, 22 Gayfield Square, Edinburgh, 1831, husband of **Sarah Lifman** or **Lipman.** [FJC. 39]

LIPMAN, JULIA, aged 15, born in Midlothian, **Amelia Lipman,** aged 14, born in Midlothian, **Godfrey Lipman,** aged 13, born in Midlothian, **Lenia Lipman,** aged 8, born in Midlothian, **Rebeckah Lipman,** aged 7, born in Midlothian, **John Lipman,** aged 5, born in Midlothian, and **Sarah Lipman,** aged 5, born in Midlothian, in Howe Street, Edinburgh, 1841. [Census]

LIPMAN, M., born 1809 in London, a quill dresser, 20 Mason Street, Glasgow, wife **Rachel** born 1810 in Edinburgh, daughters **Rose** born 1843 in Glasgow, and **Amelia** born 1847 in Glasgow, 1851. [Census]

LIPMAN and HAMEL, merchants, 17 Cowgate, Dundee, 1846. [DD]

LIPPMAN, MOSS, 1837. [NRS.CS311.774]

LIPMAN, MOSES, born 1811 in England, a traveller, 35 Govan Street, Glasgow, with **Rachel Lipman,** born 1811 in Scotland, **Joseph Lipman,** born 1837 in Scotland, and **Sarah Lipman,** born 1840 in Scotland, 1841. [Census]

LIPMAN, SAMUEL, born 1829 in England, an ornament manufacturer, 41 Adelphi Street, Glasgow, 1851. [Census]

LIPMAN, SARAH, wife of **John Lipman,** died 17 December -595, aged 60 or 69. [JBGE]

LISENHEIM, JACOB H., born in Schlank, Poland, 1785, from Konigsberg, landed in Gravesend, settled in Edinburgh by 1813, a jeweller and silversmith at Palmer's Buildings, 17 West Nicolson, Edinburgh, 1824, at 11 Roxburgh Street, 1832, at 8 Roxburgh Street, 1833. [FJC.5/39] [EBR:SL115]

LISENHEIM, JOHN, a merchant at 75 Nicolson Street, Edinburgh, 1818, and at 1 West Richmond Street, Edinburgh, 1819. [FJC.40]

LISENHEIM, MOSES HENRY, jeweller at 156 Pleasance, Edinburgh, 1820; minister, Hebrew teacher and schochet, 43 High Street, Glasgow from 1823; 1821. [FJC.40][NRS.CS231.L4.31][SCJ.19]

LISIMAN, SARAH, probate 1705 Bristol.[TNA]

LITHMAN, CATHARINE, born 1757, a spinster from London, an indentured servant bound from London to New York aboard the Adventurer in 1775. [TNA.T47.9/11]

LITTMAN, GEORGE, on Nevis, 1708. [TNAS.C0.152-157]

LOBATTO, DEBORAH, resettled on Nevis, 1712. [JTP.1709-1715.386]

LOBATTO, JACOB, an alien, was granted denization 2 February 1695. [S.P.Dom.Warrant book.40.16]

LOBATTO, SARAH, resettled on Nevis, 1712. [JTP.1709-1715.383]

LOBO, DANIEL, a notary public in Birmingham, 1780

LOPEZ, ABRAHAM, from Barbados aboard the ship Hope bound for London in 1679. [TNA.CO1]

LOPES, ABRAHAM, in St Michael's parish, Barbados, 1679. [TNA.CO1.44.47]; with 2 children {?} in St Michael's 1680. [TNA.CO1]

LOPAZ, ABRAHAM, a merchant, with his wife **Rebecca,** sons **Joseph, Isaac, Gabriel,** and daughters **Rachael, Hester, Leah, Sarah,** in the parish of St Katherine, Coleman, London, 1695. [LRS.1966.189]

LOPEZ, ABRAHAM RODRIGUES, a merchant, died on 13 March 1788 in St Jago de la Vega, Jamaica. [GM.58.933]

LOPEZ, ANDREW, a grant of denization, 11 October 1687, [Patent Roll 1 Jas ii]; a merchant in London, 1695. [ActsPCCol.II.288]; a merchant in London, 1698. [TNA.HCA.81.Lopez, versus, Anthony]

LOPEZ, DAVID, an alien, a grant of denization, 25 October 1667. [Patent Roll, 19 Car ii]

LOPEZ, ELIAH, in St Michael's parish, Barbados, 1679. [TNA.CO1.44.47]; with 5 children {?} in St Michael's 1680. [TNA.CO1]

LOPEZ, ISAAC, in St Michael's parish, Barbados, 1679. [TNA.CO1.44.47]

LOPEZ, JACOB, in the parish of St James, Duke's Place, London, 1695. [LRS.1966.189]

LOPES, MANASSE, born in Jamaica, settled in England, a convert, a baronet in 1802 and an MP by 1806.........

LOPEZ, MANUEL, a merchant in London, 1695. [ActsPCCol.II.288]

LOPES, MORDECAI R., in Jamaica, probate 1796, PCC. [TNA]

LOPES, MOSES PARRO, probate Jamaica, 1733. [BM. Add. MS.21,931]

LOPEZ, RACHELL, in St Michael's parish, Barbados, 1679. [TNA.CO1.44.47]; with 4 children {?} in St Michael's 1680. [TNA.CO1]

LOPEZ, RODRINGES ABRAHAM, probate Jamaica, 1741. [BM.Add MS 21,931]

LOPEZ, RODRINGES M., probate Jamaica, 1743. [BM.Add MS 21,931]

LOPEZ, SARAH, a widow, in the parish of St Katherine Cree, London, 1695. [LRS.1966.189]

LOPES, SIMON, was granted a pass to travel from England to Holland on 6 April 1705. [TNA.SP44.390.417]

LOPEZ, TELLES ABRAHAM, from Barbados aboard the ship Recovery to Jamaica in 1679. [TNA.CO1]

LOUSADA, ARON BARON, an alien, a grant of denization, 20 August 1675. [Patent Roll, 27 Car ii.8]

LOUSADA, AARON BARUCH, executor of John Woolery, also Rachel Baruch Lousada his widow, 1767/1769. [ActsPCCol.V.118]

LOUSADA, ABIGAIL BARUH, in Barbados, probate 1790 PCC.[TNA]

LOUZADA, ABRAHAM BARUH, an alien, a merchant, a grant of denization, 20 April 1672. [Patent Roll, 24 Car ii, part 4]

LOUSADA, ANTONIO, an alien, a grant of denization, 10 June 1675. [Patent Roll, 27 Car ii part 8]

LOUSADA, AARON BARUH, a petitioner in Jamaica, 1752. [ActsPCCol. 1745-1766.151]

LOUZADA, ARON, in Jamaica, probate 1768, PCC. [TNA]

LOUSADA, DANIEL BARUH, in Jamaica, probate 1769, PCC. [TNA]

LOUSADA, DAVID BARUH, a grant of denization, 18 April 1664, [Patent Roll, 18 April 1664]; a free denizen of Barbados, 1669. [ActsPCCol.I. 534]

LOUSADA, EMANUEL BARUH, formerly a merchant in Jamaica, now of Stoke Newington, Middlesex, an indenture, 1802, [Car.2.330/367/369; Car.3.157]; probate 1807, PCC. [TNA]

LOUSADA, JACOB BARUH, in Jamaica, probate 1752, PCC. [TNA]

LOUZADA, LEAH, in Barbados, probate 1765 PCC. [TNA]

LOUSADA, MOSES BARUTH, an alien, was granted denization on 14 December 1694. [S.P.Dom.Warrant book.39.124]

LOUSADA, RACHEL BARUH, a widow in Jamaica by 1775. [Car.3.155]; probate 1807, PCC. [TNA]

LOUSADA, SARAH, in Barbados, probate 1788 PCC. [TNA]

LOUSADA, versus WOOLERY, HARDYMAN, an appeal from Jamaica, 1770. [ActsPCCol.unbound papers#828]

LUBATCHEWSKY, Dr J., from St Petersburg, landed in Gravesend in 1819, settled in Edinburgh by 1820. [EBR:SL115][FJC.5]

LUBECK, SOLOMAN, 1828. [NRS.CS230.L6.23]

LUCAS, ISRAEL L., born 1832, died 20 April 1910. [Piershill MI, Edinburgh]

LUCAS, L., born 1841, died 24 January 1913. [Piershill MI, Edinburgh]

LUCENA, ABRAHAM RODRIGUES, a merchant 'born in foreign parts', a grant of denization, 8 October 1663. [Patent Roll, 15 Car i.16]

LUCENY, SAMUEL, with his wife Rebecca, son Jacob, and daughters Rachel, Leah, in the parish of St Katherine Coleman, London, 1695. [LRS.1966.190]

LUIS, T. H., of Jaffe Brothers, house 6 Hawkhill Place, Dundee, 1856. [DD]

LUSSANE, SAMUEL, with his wife Rebecca, daughter Rachel, and son Jacob, in the parish of St James, Duke's Place, London, 1695. [LRS. 1966.191]

LUTMAN, JOSIAH, with his wife Susan, sons Josiah, John, and daughters Joan, Johana, in the parish of St Martin Outwich, London, 1659. [LRS.1966.191]

LYON, ABRAHAM, with his wife Elizabeth, son Isaac, and daughters Rachel, Leah, in the parish of St Katherine Cree, London, 1695. [LRS. 1966.191]

LYON, ABRAHAM, a quill manufacturer, 35 North Richmond Street, Edinburgh, 1834. [FJC.41]

LYON, ABRAHAM VALLERY, fourth son of **James** and **Louisa Lyon,** died on 3 November 1837 aged 11 months. [Braid Place MI, Edinburgh]

LYON, BENJAMIN, in Jamaica, probate 1780, PCC. [TNA]

LYON, BENJAMIN, graduated MD in Aberdeen, 1783. [CJ]

LYON, BENJAMIN, third son of the late **Benjamin Lyon** in Jamaica, died in Spanish Town, Jamaica, 5 September 1800. [GM.70.1107]

??LYON, DAVID, jr., an apothecary, and agent for the Age Assurance Company, 46 Wellgate, Dundee, house 21 Dudhope Crescent, Dundee, 1853. [DD]

LYON, ELIZABETH ANNE, daughter of the late **Benjamin Lyon** in Jamaica, married J. Kerr Jordan, son of the late Captain J. Dudley Jordan, and grandson of **Jacob Jordan** in Lower Canada, in Clifton on 10 August 1845. [GM.NS24.50]

LYON, HANNAH, a widow, with sons **Joseph, Steven,** and daughters **Hannah, Jane, Mary,** in the parish of Christ Church, London, 1695. [LRS.1966.191]

LYON, HANNAH, a German Jew, was granted a pass to travel from England to Holland, 22 March 1706. [TNA.SP44.390.404]

LYON, HANA, aged 40, born in Amsterdam, landed in London, settled in Edinburgh by 1798. [FJC.5][EBR:SL115]

LYON, HENRY, born 1805, died 1878, husband of **Rebecca Bright,** parents of **Charlotte Lyon** [1837-1882]. [Deane Road Cemetery, Liverpool]

LYON, HENRY WALTER, died 8 November 1832 aged 4 years 1 month 20 days. [JBGE]

LYON, HERMAN, aged 50, born in Maghedorf, Germany, a dentist, settled in Edinburgh by 1788. [EBR.SL115]

LYON, HERMAN, from Prizal in Brabant, landed in London, settled in Edinburgh by 1794. [FJC.5][EBR:SL115]

LYON, HERMAN, from Prussia, a dentist and 'corn operator' [ie a chiropodist] in Edinburgh from 1788, 'opposite the Linen Hall, Canongate, 1794-1800, buried on Calton Hill, Edinburgh.[ED 1794-6 and 1799-1800][EBR:1793] [OSJ.10]; according to the *Newcastle Courant* 'Lyon Hermann dentist of Edinburgh, married **Mrs H. Pollack**, a widow from London' in Sunderland on 3 December 1791.

LYON, ISAAC, a mariner in London, 1684. [GLRO.MR.E593]

LYON, J. W., goldsmith, jeweller, and diamond setter, 25 Princes Street, Edinburgh, 1833, at 89 George Street, Edinburgh, in 1840. [FJC. 39]; **James Walter Lyon,** born 1801 in England, a merchant, 89 George Street, Edinburgh, wife **Louisa Lyon,** born 1806 in England, son **Charles James Lyon,** born 1827 in England, son **Nathan David Lyon,** born 1830 in England, daughter **Mary Miriam Lyon,** born 1837 in Midlothian, and son **Isodor Bernadotte Lyon,** born 1839 in Midlothian, also **Rosina Lyon,** born 1796 in England, 1841. [Census]

LYON, JACOB, a German Jew, was granted a pass to travel from England to Holland, 22 March 1706. [TNA.SP44.390.404]

LYON, JOSEPH, an apprentice, in the parish of St Michael le Querne, London, 1695. [LRS.1966.191]

LYON, JOSEPH, a poor Jew, was granted a pass to travel from England to Holland, 23 October 1706. [TNA.SP44.393.185]

LYON, JOSEPH, a pawnbroker and silversmith in Hull 1829. [HCA.C.DJC]

LYON, JOSEPH, a saddler, High Street, Dundee; Lyon's Buildings, Hawkhill, Dundee, 1837. [DD]

LYON, M., a straw hat maker, 10 Charles Street, Edinburgh, 1819. [FJC. 40]

LYONS, MORRIS, in Glasgow, 1840s. [SCJ.22]

LYON, MOSES, a bachelor, in the parish of St James, Duke's Place, London, 1695. [LRS.1966.192]

LYON, RACHEL, a widow, in the parish of St James, Duke's Place, London, 1695. [LRS.1966.192]

LYON, ROSA, first daughter of **James** and **Louise Lyon,** died 28 June 18....., aged 3- years 7 months. [JBGE]

LYONS, versus LYONS, in Antigua, an appeal to the Privy Council Colonial, 1717. [Acts P.C.Col. 1727, #379]

MACHER, MOISES, a German Jew, was granted a pass to travel from England to Holland, 8 November 1705. [TNA.SP44.390.330]

MADENA, ABRAHAM, a militiaman in Barbados, 1679. [TNA.CO1.44.47]

MADENA, JACOB, a bachelor, in the parish of St Lawrence Cree, London, 1695. [LRS.1966.192]

MAIERS, REBECCA, a poor Jew, was granted a pass to travel from England to Holland, 10 October 1706. [TNA.SP44.393.178]

MAINZER, Dr JOSEPH, a decree, 1849. [NRS.SC39.17.11712]

MALADY, JACOB LOPAS, with his wife **Rachel Lopas,** in the parish of St Andrew Undershaft, London, 1695. [LRS.1966.193]

MANBY, AARON, a saddler in Kingston, Jamaica, an indenture 1779, [Car.3.24]; probate 1780, PCC. [TNA]

MANSELL, NEHEMIAH, a bachelor, in the parish of St Michael le Querne, London, 1695. [LRS.1966.194]

MANSFEILD, BENJAMIN, with his wife **Margaret,** and son **Nathan,** in the parish of St Michael, Cornhill, London, 1695. [LRS.1966.194]

MANSFELT, MICHAEL, a bachelor, in the parish of St Michael, Crooked Lane, London, 1695. [LRS.1966.194]

MANUEL, BENJAMIN, an apprentice, in the parish of St Leonard, Foster Lane, London, 1695. [LRS.1966.194]

MANUELL, ISRAEL, a bachelor, in the parish of St Katherine Cree, London, 1695. [LRS.1966.194]

MARBE, ABRAHAM MOSES, born in Lissar, Grand Duchy of Posen, Prussia, a manufacturing chemist, died 1859. [Betholom MI, Birmingham]

MARCUS, ALEXANDER, a German Jew, was granted a pass to travel from England to Holland, 2 July 1706. [TNA.SP44.393.22]

MARCUS, MOISES, a German Jew, was granted a pass to travel from England to Holland, 11 February 1706. [TNA.SP44.390.378]

MARCUS, MOISES, a German Jew, was granted a pass to travel from England to Holland, 2 July 1706. [TNA.SP44.393.22]

MARCUS, MOSES, late of Brigstock, Northamptonshire, formerly in New York, died in London on 25 November 1852. [GM.NS39.215]

MARGET, JOSEPH, with his wife **Rebecca,** in the parish of St Leonard, Foster Lane, London, 1695. [LRS.1966.195]

MARGOLIOTH, NAPTHALI, from Vienna, 1603, see Otto, Julius Conradus.

MARKES, BENDICK, with his wife **Rachel,** in the parish of St Andrew Undershaft, London, 1695. [LRS.1966.195]

MARKES, DAVID, with his wife, and son **Levi,** in the parish of St Andrew Undershaft, London, 1695. [LRS.1966.195]

MARKS, ISAAC, born 1791 in Scotland, a quill manufacturer, St Andrew Street, Dumfries, 1841. [Census]

MARKS, JOSEPH, born 1784 'in foreign parts', a watchmaker, 7 Richmond Place, Edinburgh, 1841. [Census]

MARKS, MARY, born 1796 in Ireland, Lyons Lane, Port Glasgow, with **James Marks,** laborer, born 1821 in Ireland, **Nathaniel Marks,** born 1829 in Ireland, hand loom weaver, **Jacob Marks,** born 1831 in Ireland, **Rosy Marks,** born 1825 in Ireland, **Mary Marks,** born 1835 in Ireland, 1841. [Census]

MARKES, MOSES, in the parish of St Andrew Undershaft, London, 1695. [LRS.1966.195]

MARKES, SAMPSON, a bachelor in the parish of St James, Duke's Place, London, 1695. [LRS.1966.195]

MARKES, SOLOMON, with his wife **Judith,** in the parish of St Andrew Undershaft, London, 1695. [LRS.1966.195]

MARKES, ZACARIAH, with his wife **Rose,** and son **Samuel,** in the parish of St Andrew Undershaft, London, 1695. [LRS.1966.195]

MARLOW, ISAAC, with his wife **Esther,** and son **Isaac,** in the parish of St Clement, Eastcheap, London, 1695. [LRS.1966.195]

MARQUES, ANTONIO RODRIQUES, an alien, a grant of denization, 9 June 1688. [Patent Roll, 4 Jas ii, part 6]

MARX,........, 1812. [NRS.CS148.122]

MASS, FANNY, born 1771 'in foreign parts', Greenside Place, Edinburgh, 1841. [Census]

MASSIAS, JACOB, a planter in St Peter's parish, Barbados, 1679. [TNA.CO1.44.47]

MASSIAS, SAMUEL, probate 1747 Jamaica. [BM.Add MS 21,931]

MATTHEWS, MORRIS, born 1811 in Poland, a clothier's assistant, 6 Miller Street, Glasgow, 1851. [Census]

MAW, SOLOMON, a decree, 23 August 1848. [NRS.SC39.17.11256]

MAWSON, SAMUEL MOSES, merchant in Edinburgh, formerly in India and in America, a bankrupt 1823, son of **Jacob Moses** formerly a merchant in London, brother-in-law of **John Levitt** from London. [NRS.CS44.45.56]

MAXQUEZ, ISAQUE R., took the Oath of Association in New York, 1696. [TNA]

MAYER, MOSES, goldsmith, a receipt, Copenhagen, November 1719. [NRS.GD158.1792]

MAYERS, BENJAMIN, born 1764, a former Assemblyman, died in Tenby, Barbados, on 3 June 1854. [GM.NS42.201]

MAYOS, JOHN, with his wife **Hannah,** and daughter **Sarah,** in the parish of St Anne, Blackfriars, London, 1695. [LRS.1966.200]

MAYOS, MATTHIAS, a bachelor, in the parish of St Anne, Blackfriars, London, 1695. [LRS.1966.200]

MAZAHOD, JACOB, an alien, a grant of denization, 24 May 1677, [Patent Roll, 20 Car ii, part 8]; a bachelor, in the parish of St James, Duke Place, London, 1695. [LRS.1966.200]

MAZEY, HANNAH, in the parish of St Gregory by St Paul's, London, 1695. [LRS.1966.200]

MECHADO, ABRAHAM, a gentleman, with his wife **Sarah,** in the parish of St Katherine, Coleman, London, 1695. [LRS.1966.200]

MEDINAH, LEAH, in St Michael's parish, Barbados, 1679. [TNA.CO1.44.47]; with 7 children {?} in St Michael's 1680. [TNA.CO1]

MEERES, ABRAHAM, with his wife **Isabella,** and son **David,** in the parish of St Michael, Queenhithe, London, 1695. [LRS.1966.200]

MEFFIAT, SIMON, a merchant in Barbados, married **Deborah Bilenfaite** in 1768. [GM.38.198]

MEIER, RACHEL, late of New Palz, Ulster County, New York, probate 1820, PCC. [TNA]

MELLADA, ISAACK, a militiaman in Barbados, 1679. [TNA.CO1.44.47]

MELLADO, ISAAC HENRIQUES, an alien, a grant of denization, 10 December 1695. [Patent Roll, 7 Wm. iii, part 4]

MENDES, ABRAHAM DE SOZA, an alien in Jamaica, a grant of denization, 9 September 1670. [Patent Office, 22 Car ii]

MENDEZ, ABRAHAM, in the parish of All Hallows, London Wall, 1695. [LRS.1966.201]

MENDEZ, DANIEL, on Nevis, 1678. [TNA.CO1]

MENDES, HENRIQUE JORGE, in London 1655, later in Antwerp. [TJS.i. 72] [CalSPDom.1655.586]

MENDEZ, HONOUR, in the parish of All Hallows, London Wall, 1695. [LRS.1966.201]

MENDEZ, ISAACK, with his wife **Judith,** in the parish of St James, Duke's Place, London Wall, 1695. [LRS.1966.201]

MENDEZ, JOSEPH, an alien, a grant of denization, 25 October 1667. [Patent Roll, 19 Car ii]

MENDES, JOSEPH, a planter in St Peter's parish, Barbados, 1679. [TNA.CO1.44.47]

MENDES, JOSEPH, in Barbados, probate 1712 PCC. [TNA]

MENDEZ, LENORA, in the parish of All Hallows, London Wall, 1695. [LRS.1966.201]

MENDEZ, MENASSA, a grant of denization, 11 October 1687, [Patent Roll, 1 Jas ii]; with his wife **Deborah,** sons **Abraham, Benjamin,** and daughter **Sarah** in the parish of All Hallows, London Wall, 1695. [LRS. 1966.201]

MENDEZ, RACHEL, with three children, on Nevis, 1678. [TNA.CO1]

MENDES, SIMON, a planter in St Peter's parish, Barbados, 1679. [TNA.CO1.44.47]

MENDES, SOLOMON, in St Peter's parish, Barbados, 1679. [TNA.CO1.44.47]

MENDEZ, SOLOMON, petitioned to emigrate to the Plantations, 1680. [SPAWI.1680.1347]

MENDOOS, JACOB, with his wife **Rachel,** and daughter **Rebecca,** in the parish of St Andrew, Undershaft, London, 1695. [LRS.1966.201]

MEPHAM, ABRAHAM, a servant, in the parish of St Benet Fink, London, 1695. [LRS.1966.201]

MERANDO, EMANUEL NUNEZ, a merchant, with his wife **Abigail,** and daughters **Rachel, Hester, Sarah, Deborah, Abigail,** and son **Joseph,** in the parish of St James, Duke's Place, London, 1695. [LRS.1966.201]

MERCADO, MOSES, in St Michael's parish, Barbados, 1679. [TNA.CO1.44.47]; with 5 children {?} in St Michael's 1680. [TNA.CO1]

MERCATS, ABRAHAM, a bachelor, in the parish of St Katharine Cree, London, 1695. [LRS.1966.201]

MERCATS, SARAH, a widow, with her daughter Sarah, in the parish of St Katharine Cree, London, 1695. [LRS.1966.201]

MERENIO, SOLOMON, a bachelor, in the parish of St Andrew Undershaft, London, 1695. [LRS.1966.201]

MESAW, ISAACK, a militiaman in Barbados, 1679. [TNA.CO1.44.47]

MESIJER, ABRAHAM, took the Oath of Association in New York, 1696. [TNA]

MESQUETA, EPHRAIM, resettled on Nevis, 1712. [JTP.1709-1715.383]

MESSEWS, ISAACK, with his wife Rachel, and son Joseph, in the parish of St James, Duke's Place, London, 1695. [LRS.1966.202]

MESSIAS, BONA, with daughters Rachel and Sarah, in the parish of St James, Duke's Place, London, 1695. [LRS.1966.202]

MESSIAS, JACOB, a militiaman in Barbados, 1679. [TNA.CO1.44.47]

MESSIAS, MOSES, a perfumer, admitted as a burgess of the Canongate, Edinburgh, 29 September 1694. [Roll of Canongate Burgesses]

MESAW, ISAACK, a militiaman in Barbados, 1679. [TNA.CO1.44.47]

METZEBERG, BARNET, born 1830, died 7 August 1902. [Newington MI, Edinburgh]

METZENBURG, LEVI, in Glasgow, sequestration, 1849. [NRS.CS279.1388]

MEYERS, BARNETT, a decree, 22 January 1845. [NRS.SC39.17.9210]

MEYER, C., a silk mercer, 92 George Street, Edinburgh, 1835. [EPOD]

MEYER, JACOB, a German Jew, was granted a pass to travel from England to Holland, 25 February 1706. [TNA.SP44.390.388]

MEYER, MATHIAS, a German Jew, was granted a pass to travel from England to Holland, 23 July 1706. [TNA.SP44.393.36]

MEYER, PETER, born in Hamburg, son of Jacob Meyer and Elizabeth Meyer, a grant of naturalization, 1690. [Patent Roll, 3 Wm & Mary part 8/552]

MEYER, Sir PETER, in Barbados, probate 1728 PCC. [TNA]

MEYER, PHILIP T., born 1732, the eminent composer and professor of harp, died on 17 January 1820. [SM.85.293]

MEYERS, PRANCA, a poor Jew, was granted a pass to travel from England to Holland, 10 October 1706. [TNA.SP44.393.178]

MEYER, ROBERT M., born 1816 'in foreign parts', an agent or merchant, 4 St Andrew's Street, Dundee, 1840, 1841. [DD][Census]

MEYER, SAUL, born 1821 'in foreign parts', a merchant, High Street, Kirkcudbright, 1841. [Census]

MEYER, SOLOMON, of the Posterngate Synagogue, Hull, 1826. [HCA.C.DJC]

MEZA, ISACK, in St Michael's parish, Barbados, 1679. [TNA.CO1.44.47]; with 3 children {?} in St Michael's 1680. [TNA.CO1]

MEZA, ALONSO DE FONSECA, born in Spain, a grant of denization, 30 May 1661. [Patent Roll, 13 Car ii.16]

MEZA, JACOB DE FONSECA, born in Spain, a grant of denization, 30 May 1661. [Patent Roll, 13 Car ii.16]

MEZA, MANUEL DA FONSECA, in London, 16... [TJS.i.69]

MICHAEL, JACOB, born 1810, died 10 May 1894. [Newington MI, Edinburgh]

MICHAEL, JONAS, agent and auctioneer, 12 Candleriggs, Glasgow, 1822. [SCJ.18]

MICHAL, LEAH, born 1846, wife of Bernard Franklin, died 30 October 1918. [Newington MI, Edinburgh]

MICHAEL, LENA, born 1830, died 28 April 1896. [Newington MI, Edinburgh]

MICHAEL, MICHAEL, a mohel in Glasgow, 1824, died in October 1833. [SCJ.19/20]

MICHAEL, SAMUEL, a hammerman, was admitted as a burgess of Glasgow, July 1823. [GBR]

MICHELSON, MOSES, born 1841, died 29 April 1906 in Aberdeen. [Newington MI, Edinburgh]

MIERS, JOSEPH, in the parish of All Hallows, Barking, London, 1695. [LRS.1966.203]

MIERS, NATHAN, in the parish of St Michael, Crooked Lane, London, 1695. [LRS.1966.203]

MILIADE, ISAAC LOPEZ, an alien, a grant of denization, 30 November 1693. [Patent Roll, 5 William and Mary 4, part 2]

MINGO, JUDAH, in the parish of St Christopher le Stocks, London, 1695. [LRS.1695.205]

MIRANDA, ABRAHAM, probate 1748 Jamaica. [BM.Add MS 21,931]

MIRASSON, JOSEPH, a decree, 1845. [NRS.SC39.17.9190]

MOCATTA, ABRAHAM DE MATTAS, and his wife Esther Lamego, 1761. [Car.2.367]

MOCATO, EMANUEL, with his wife Rachel, and daughters Hesther, Rhina, Rebecca, and Sarah, in the parish of St Katherine Cree, London, 1695. [LRS.1966.205]

MOCATTA, FREDERICK DAVID, born 1828, a financier and philanthropist in London, died 1905.

MOCATO, MOSES, alias Thomas George, an alien, a grant of denization, January 1680. [Patent Office, 32 Car ii];

MOCATTA, MOSES, born 1675 in London, residing in Duke's Place, book-keeper to Francis de Cassares, a witness in the High Court of the Admiralty of England, 1698. [TNA.HCA.Vol.81, Exams.,1698]

MOCATO, REBECCA, a widow, with son Abraham, daughters Hannah, Rachel, and Rebecca, in the parish of St Katherine Cree, London, 1695. [LRS.1966.205]

MODICENA, HESTER, with daughters Judith, Abigail, and sons David, Abraham, in the parish of St James, Duke's Place, London, 1695. [LRS. 1966.205]

MOISES, ABRAHAM, a German Jew, was granted a pass to travel from England to Holland, 18 June 1706. [TNA.SP44.393.10]

MOISES, HANA, a poor Jew, was granted a pass to travel from England to Holland, 10 October 1706. [TNA.SP44.393.178]

MOISES, ISAAC, a German Jew, was granted a pass to travel from England to Holland, 3 January 1706. [TNA.SP44.390.362]

MOISES, ISAAC, a German Jew, was granted a pass to travel from England to Holland, 22 April 1706. [TNA.SP44.390.436]

MOISES, JOSEPH, a German Jew, was granted a pass to travel from England to Holland, 26 August 1706. [TNA.SP44.393.70]

MOISES, LEVI, a German Jew, was granted a pass to travel from England to Holland, 28 February 1706. [TNA.SP44.390.390]

MOISES, MARCUS, a German Jew, was granted a pass to travel from England to Holland, 11 February 1706. [TNA.SP44.390.378]

MOISES, PHILIPPE, a German Jew, was granted a pass to travel from England to Holland, 25 September 1706. [TNA.SP44.393.100]

MOISES, RECHEL, a German Jew, was granted a pass to travel from England to Holland, 3 January 1706. [TNA.SP44.390.362]

MOISES, TOBIA, a German Jew, was granted a pass to travel from England to Holland, 5 April 1706. [TNA.SP44.390.415a]

MOLACE, ABRAHAM, a servant, in the parish of All Hallows, Barking, London, 1695. [LRS.1966.205]

MOLEEW, RACHEL, with daughter Hester, in the parish of St James, Duke's Place, London, 1695. [LRS.1966.205]

MOLLWO, HERMAN, a flax merchant, Meadow House, Dundee, 1837; a flax spinner, 43 East Cowgate, house Springbank, Dundee, 1840; 20 Springfield Place, Dundee, 1853. [DD]

MONSANTO, ESTHER M., in Jamaica, probate 1795, PCC. [TNA]

MONTEFIORE, JUDAH ISRAEL, graduated MD from King's College, Aberdeen, on 27 January 1824, recommended by Dr **John Meyer.** [KCA. 159]

MONTEFIOR, RAPHAEL, a German Jew, was granted a pass to travel from England to Holland, 7 August 1706. [TNA.SP44.393.52]

MONTEFIORE, ..., son of **Joseph Meyer Montefiore,** was born at Worth Park, Sussex, on 10 October 1860. [GM.NS.IX.543]

MONTOR, JACOB, a German Jew, was granted a pass to travel from England to Holland, 24 June 1706. [TNA.SP44.393.14]

MOON, ABRAHAM, with his wife **Sarah,** in the parish of St Andrew Undershaft, London, 1695. [LRS.1966.206]

MORCAT, ISAAC, with his wife **Rachel** and son **David,** German Jews, were granted a pass to travel from England to Holland, 23 July 1706. [TNA.SP44.393.61]

MORRENA, ..., a widow, with her daughters **Hannah, Rebecca,** and **Hesther,** and son **Elias,** in the parish of St Andrew Undershaft, London, 1695. [LRS.1966.208]

MOSELY, MOSS, a merchant in Edinburgh, 1825. [FJC.6/41]

MOSES, A., a leather manufacturer in Fleur de Lys Street, Spitalfields, London, bankrupt, 1820. [SM.86.284]

MOSES, AARON, with his wife **Rose,** and daughter **Leah,** in the parish of St James, Duke's Place, London, 1695. [LRS.1966.209]

MOSES, D., born in Amsterdam, landed at Gravesend, settled in Edinburgh by 1803, an umbrella maker in Canongate. [EBR:SL115][FJC. 5]

MOSES, DAVID MORTON, an assessor of income tax, 17 St Patrick Square, Edinburgh, 1859. [ELD]

MOSES, ESTHER, [wife?] of Mr **Philip Levy** of Edinburgh, 32 Castle Street, Edinburgh, 1806, at 6 Castle Street, Edinburgh, 1816-1821. [FJC.41][JBGE]

MOSES, JACOB, formerly a merchant in London later in Edinburgh, a haberdasher, 30 Lothian Road, Edinburgh, 1823; an agent or navy agent in 1825; a decreet, 1826. [NRS.CS44.95.15][FJC.41]

MOSES, JOHN, an indentured servant bound from London to Pennsylvania in 1725. [CLRO]

MOSES, JONAS, a merchant in Emden, 1732. [NRS.AC9.1174]

MOSES, JOSEPH, formerly in Gun Square, London, lately in Charlestown, USA, administration to relict **Sarah Moses,** 1803, PCC. [TNA]

MOSES, LYON, aged 24, a lapidary from London, an indentured servant aboard the <u>Dolphin</u> bound from London to Philadelphia in 1774. [TNA.T47.9/11]

MOSES, MARK, aged 23, a schoolmaster from London, emigrated from London aboard the <u>Neptune</u> bound for Maryland in 1775. [TNA.T47.9/11]

MOSES, MARTHA, 1 Porchester Terrace North, London, died 14 November 1861, intestate, inventory, Commissary of Edinburgh. [NRS]

MOSES, MICHAEL, a bachelor, in the parish of All Hallows, Bread Street, London, 1695. [LRS.1966.209]

MOSES, SIMON, a merchant in Emden, 1732. [NRS.AC9.1174]

MOSES, SOLOMAN, a merchant in Emden, 1732. [NRS.AC9.1174]

MOSES, WILLIAM, a merchant in Glasgow, a deed, 18 January 1813. [NAS.RS27.5.252]

MOSES, WILLIAM, a tailor, 9 Earl Grey Street, Edinburgh, 1835. [EPOD]

MOSES, SON, & DAVIS, decrees, 1852/1855. [NRS.SC39.17.12894/13597]

MOSIAS, MOSES, merchant in Edinburgh, 14 December 1698. [EBR]

MOSS, BENJAMIN, born 1796 in England, a man servant in Culhorn House, Wigtownshire, with **Benjamin Moss,** born 1817 in Scotland, a man servant, 1841. [Census]

MOSS, JOHN, and his son **Isaac,** were granted a pass to travel from England to Holland on 22 July 1705. [TNA.SP44.393.35]

MOSS, LEWIS, 1837. [NRS.CS235.M58.3]

MOSSES, WILLIAM, tailor, 74 Thistle Street, Edinburgh, 1858. [EPOD]

MOYSE, SHADRACH, a Customs officer, was admitted as a burgess and guilds-brother of Edinburgh on 24 November 1762, [EBR]; in Princes Street, Edinburgh, 1780; a Commissioner at 21 Princes Street, Edinburgh, 1806-1811. [Edinburgh Almanacs, 1780/1806/1810][EBR] [OSJ.10]

MUGGADORY, PENTALIA, a merchant, with his wife **Rachel,** and daughter **Hester,** in the parish of St James, Duke's Place, London, 1695. [LRS.1966.210]

MUSQUETA, EPHRAIM, a planter, resettled on Nevis, 1712. [JTP. 1712.386]

MYERS, JOSEPH HART, born in New York 1758, graduated MD from Edinburgh University in 1779. [OSJ.10]

MYERS, JOSEPH, born 1846, husband of **Julia,** died 12 April 1911. [Newington MI, Edinburgh]

MYERS, JULIA, born 1850, widow of **Joseph Myers,** died 8 August 1941. [Newington MI, Edinburgh]

MYERS, LEVI, from Carolina, graduated MD from Glasgow University in 1787. [RGG.466]

MYERS, NAPTHALI H., Warden of the Great Synagogue, John Street, America Square, London, 1771, a letter. [Cal.H.O.pp.1771.973]

NAMIAS, DAVID, an alien in Barbados, a grant of denization, 27 December 1662. [Patent Roll.14 Car.ii.7]; in St Michael's parish, Barbados, 1679. [TNA.CO1.44.47]; with 9 children {?} in St Michael's 1680. [TNA.CO1]

NAPTHALY, ISAAC, an alien, was granted denization, 10 August 1699. [Patent Roll, 11 William III, pt.6.]

NATAN, DANIEL, a poor Jew, was granted a pass to travel from England to Holland, 21 October 1706. [TNA.SP44.393.179]

NATAN, MOISES, a poor Jew, was granted a pass to travel from England to Holland, 21 October 1706. [TNA.SP44.393.179]

NATHAN, BERNHARD, a German Jew, was granted a pass to travel from England to Holland, 5 August 1706. [TNA.SP44.393.50]

NATHAN, DANIEL, a German Jew, was granted a pass to travel from England to Holland, 11 April 1706. [TNA.SP44.390.422]

NATHAN, GEORGE, and his wife **Elizabeth,** in the parish of All Hallows the Great, London, 1695. [LRS.1966.212]

NATHAN, NATHANIAEL, born 1847, died 5 April 1920. [Piershill MI, Edinburgh]

NATHAN, PHINEAS, 1839. [NRS.CS271.52830]

NATHAN, ROSE, spouse of **Henry Daniel** a glass cutter and engraver in Edinburgh, process of divorce, 1790. [NRS.CC8.6.853]

NAURRO, SAMUEL, in St Michael's parish, Barbados, 1679. [TNA.CO1.44.47]

NAVARRO, AARON, a grant of denization, 2 August 1661. [Patent Office, 13 Car ii]; in St Michael's parish, Barbados, 1679. [TNA.CO1.44.47]; with 7 children {?} in St Michael's 1680. [TNA.CO1]

NAVARE, ABRAHAM, with his wife **Hester,** sons **Abraham, Isaack,** and **Jacob,** in the parish of St James, Duke's Place, London, 1695. [LRS. 1966.212]

NAVARE, EMANUEL, with his wife **Rachel,** in the parish of St James, Duke's Place, London, 1695. [LRS.1966.212]

NAVARRO, ISAAC, a merchant in Barbados, a grant of denization, in February 1670. [Patent Roll, 22 Car ii]

NAVARE, JACOB, with his wife **Sarah,** son **Moses,** and daughter **Rachel,** in the parish of St James, Duke's Place, London, 1695. [LRS. 1966.212]

NAVARO, JUDITH, in St Michael's parish, Barbados, 1679. [TNA.CO1.44.47]; with 2 children{?} in St Michael's 1680. [TNA.CO1]

NAVARRO, SAMUEL, a militiaman in Barbados, 1679. [TNA.CO1.44.47]; with 4 children {?} in St Michael's 1680. [TNA.CO1]

NEBARO, SABATINI, with his wife **Sarah,** and son **Isaac,** in the parish of St Katherine Cree, London, 1695. [LRS.1695.212]

NEBLIT, ELIZABETH, a servant, in the parish of All Hallows the Less, London, 1695. [LRS.1695.212]

NEPVEN, PETER, a bachelor, in the parish of St Dunstan in the East, London, 1695. [LRS.1966.212]

NEUSTADT, DAVID SIMON, was granted a passport to travel from Hull to Hamburg, 17 February 1800. [HCA.C.BRE.7.3.18]

NEZEREAU, ELIAS, in Jamaica, probate 1709, PCC. [TNA]

NEZRO, ELIAS, a bachelor and a merchant, in the parish of St Margaret, Lothbury, London, 1695. [LRS.1966.214]

NICHOLAS, ISAAC, a collector, with his wife **Sarah,** in the parish of St Michael le Querne, London, 1695. [LRS.1966.214]

NOARE, ISAACK, a militiaman in Barbados, 1679. [TNA.CO1.44.47]

NOGUERA, ANDREW ALUES, an alien, was granted denization, 30 July 1679. [Patent Roll, 31 Car II, part 8]

NORWICH, MYER, born 1772, died 18 October 1857. [Betholom MI, Birmingham]

NOSSA, ABRAHAM, a bachelor, in the parish of St Dionis Backchurch, London, 1695. [LRS.1966.216]

NOY, HESTER, in St Michael's parish, Barbados, 1679. [TNA.CO1.44.47]; with 2 children {?} in St Michael's 1680. [TNA.CO1]

NOY, ISACC, in St Michael's parish, Barbados, 1679. [TNA.CO1.44.47]; with 6 children {?} in St Michael's 1680. [TNA.CO1]

NUNES, CORDOZO ISAAC, probate 1741 Jamaica. [BM.Add MS 21,931]

NUNES, JACOB FRANCO, in St Michael's parish, Barbados, 1679, [TNA.CO1.44.47]; with 4 children {?} in St Michael's 1680. [TNA.CO1]; a grant of denization, 11 October 1687. [Patent Roll, 1 Jas ii]

NUNES, MOSES, with his wife Sarah, sons Abraham, Isaac, David, brother Jacob, and daughters Hester, Rachel, in the parish of St Helen, London, 1695. [LRS.1966.217]

NUNES, NUNO FERNANDES, a merchant in London, 1695. [ActsPCCol.II.288]

NUNES, RACHEL, in Barbados, probate 1756 PCC. [TNA]

NUNEZ, ABRAHAM, an alien, a grant of denization, 31 October 1685. [Patent Roll, 1 James ii.15]

NUNEZ, BENJAMIN, with his wife Rachel, sons Abraham, Aaron, Emanuel, and daughters Hester, Hannah, Rebecca, Katherine, Abigail, and Leah, in the parish of St James, Duke's Place, London, 1695. [LRS.1966.217]

NUNEZ, DAVID, a jeweller and a widower, in St James Place, London, 1695. [LRS.1966.217]

NUNEZ, ISAAC R., in Jamaica, probate 1793, PCC. [TNA]

NUNEZ, MANUEL RODRIGUES, in London 16... [TJS.I.69]

OBEDIENTE, ABRAHAM, in St Michael's parish, Barbados, 1679. [TNA.CO1.44.47]; with 2 children {?} in St Michael's 1680. [TNA.CO1]

OBIN, ABRAHAM, in the parish of St Martin Outwich, London, 1695. [LRS.1966.217]

OBJENTI-ELIAS, PATCHDIEL, an alien in Barbados, a grant of denization, 27 December 1662. [Patent Roll, 14 Car.ii.7]

OLIVERO, ELIAS, a bachelor, in the parish of St James, Duke's Place, London, 1695. [LRS.1966.218]

OPPENHEIM, ABRAHAM, born Whitechapel, London, 1773, an optician in Tower Hamlets, London, 1841, son **Joseph Oppenheim,** born in Belgium 1799, an optician and tobacconist, son **Emanuel Oppenheim,** born Belgium 1811, a jeweller, daughter **Fanny Oppenheim,** born Stepney 1825. [Census]

OPPENHEIM, ALEXANDER, decrees, 1844. [NRS.SC39.17.9513/8569/8700]

OPPENHEIM, HENRY, decrees, 1831/1833. [NRS.SC39.17. 622/2504/2597]

OPPENHEIM, MICHAEL, born Prussia 1795, a Hebrew minister, 2 Caledonia Street, Liverpool, 1851, wife **Martha Oppenheim,** born Middlesex 1798, daughter Rebecca, born Liverpool, 1834. [Census]

OPPENHEIM, MICHAEL, decrees, 1833/1834/1835. [NRS.SC39.17.2171/2636/3309]

OPPENHEIM, MOSES, 1798. [NRS.CS229.O.1.46]

OPPENHEIM, PHILIP C., a decree, 24 April 1839. [NRS.SC39.17.5402]

OPPENHEIM, WALTER, decrees, 1844/1845. [NRS.SC39.17.8824/9570]

OSLAND, NEHEMIAH, with his wife **Jane,** and daughter **Jane,** in the parish of St Martin, Ludgate, London, 1695. [LRS.1966.219]

OTTO, HENRY, a decree, 1830. [NRS.SC39.17.385]

OTTO, JULIUS CONRADUS, Professor of Hebrew at Altdorf, from Vienna, Professor of Hebrew and Oriental Languages at Edinburgh University in 1641, died about 1649. [ERBE.1655-1665.34][OSJ.1]

PACHICO, JACOB, a militiaman in St Michael's parish, Barbados, 1679. [TNA.CO1.44.47]; with 5 children {?} in St Michael's 1680. [TNA.CO1]

PACHECO, REBECAH, with 2 children{?} in St Michael's 1680. [TNA.CO1]

PACHO, MOSES ISRAEL, in Barbados, grant of denization, 27 December 1662. [Patent Roll.14 Car.ii.7]

PACIFICO, EMMANUEL, in London, graduated MD from King's College, Aberdeen, on 25 June 1817, proposed by Dr **Myers.** [KCA.154]

PALACHE, MORDECAH, in St Michael's parish, Barbados, 1679. [TNA.CO1.44.47]; with 1 child{?} in St Michael's 1680. [TNA.CO1]

PALATINATE, HIGHAM, a quill-maker in Bristol, 1793. [Bristol Directory, 1793/1794]

PALPERMAN, AARON, a book-keeper from Buckinghamshire, emigrated from London aboard the <u>Elizabeth</u> bound for Virginia, 1773. [TNA.T47.9/11]

PARMINTER, ISRAEL, and his wife **Hannah,** a lease in Bristol, 1734. [BRO.20122/18]

PASS, DAVID, with his wife **Hester,** and daughters **Sarah, Rachel,** in the parish of St James, Duke's Place, London, 1695. [LRS.1966.225]

PASTANA, ABRAHAM, with his wife **Rebecca,** sons **Isack** and **Josua,** in the parish of St James, Duke's Place, London, 1695. [LRS.1966,225]

PAVIA, JAMES, an alien, a grant of denization, January 1684. [Patent Roll, 36 Car ii.6]

PAVIA, JUDITH, in the parish of All Hallows, London Wall, 1695. [LRS. 1966.225]

PAVIA, REBECCA, in the parish of All Hallows, London Wall, 1695. [LRS. 1966.225]

PECHECO, AARON, with his wife **Hesther,** son **Abraham,** and daughter **Sarah,** in the parish of St Katherine Cree, London, 1695. [LRS. 1966.227]

PECHECO, HESTHER, a widow, in the parish of St Katherine Cree, London, 1695. [LRS.1966.227]

PEIRIERA, BENJAMIN, a Jew in Surinam, petitioned to go to Jamaica, 1676. [SPAWI.1676.818.i]

PEIRIERA, DAVID, a Jew in Surinam, petitioned to go to Jamaica, 1676. [SPAWI.1676.818.i]

PEIRIERA, JACOB, a Jew in Surinam, petitioned to go to Jamaica, 1676. [SPAWI.1676.818.i]

PEIXTO, MOSES, an alien, was granted denization, 4 November 1699. [Patent Roll, 11 William III, pt.3.]

PELOQUIN, JACOB, a merchant trading between Bristol and New York, 1717. [TNA.E190.1181.1]

PENCO, DAVID, an alien, a grant of denization, 30 November 1693. [Patent Roll, 5 William and Mary 4, part 2]

PENHEIRO, ISAAC, a planter, on Nevis 1708, [TNA.CO152-157]; resettled on Nevis, 1712. [JTP.1712.386]

PERCIRA, JOSEPH, with his wife **Rachel,** in the parish of St Dionis Backchurch, London, 1695. [LRS.1966.229]

PERARA, ISAAC, in St Michael's parish, Barbados, 1679. [TNA.CO1.44.47]; with 2 children {?} in St Michael's 1680. [TNA.CO1]

PERERA, MANUEL LOPES, an alien, was granted denization, 30 July 1679. [Patent Roll, 31 Car II, part 8]

PERERA, MANUELL, with his wife **Leah,** son **David,** and daughters **Leah, Hester. Rebecca,** and **Hannah,** in the parish of All Hallows, London Wall, 1695. [LRS.1966.229]

PEREIRA, ABIGAIL, in Jamaica, probate 1798, PCC. [TNA]

PEREIRA, BENJAMIN MENDES, in Jamaica, probate 1802, PCC. [TNA]

PEREIRA, ISAAC MENDES, in Jamaica, probate 1793, PCC. [TNA]

PEREYRA, MANUEL LOPEZ, an alien, a grant of denization, 9 June 1688. [Patent Roll, 4 Jas ii, part 6]

PEREYRA, MOSES, a merchant in Barbados, a grant of denization, 17 February 1671. [Patent Roll, 23 Car ii.5]

PERETZ, S. M., a quill pen manufacturer, Pilgrim Street, Newcastle, 1823. [Newcastle Directory]

PEREZ, LEAH, a widow, in the parish of St James, Duke's Place, London, 1695. [LRS.1966.229]

PEREZ, SARAH, a widow, with son **Isaack,** and daughter **Rachel,** in the parish of St James, Duke's Place, London, 1695. [LRS.1966.229]

PEREIRA, ABRAHAM, an alien, a grant of denization, 30 September 1668. [Patent Roll, 20 Car ii]

PERIERA, ABRAM, a free denizen of Barbados, 1669. [ActsPCCol.I.534]

PERIERA, DANIEL, probate 1748 Jamaica. [BM. Add MS 21,931]

PERIERA, ISAAC, a Jew in Surinam, petitioned to go to Jamaica and settle there, 1676. [SPAWI.1676.825]

PERIERA, JOACHIM BER., from Brazil, graduated MD from Edinburgh University, 1815. [EMG.50]

PEREIRA, MENASEH BENJAMIN, an alien, was granted denization 14 December 1694. [Cal.S.P.Dom.Warrant book.39.124]

PEREIRA, MENASSAH, probate 1741 Jamaica. [BM.Add MS 21,931]

PEREIRA, SARAH, probate 1750 Jamaica. [BM. Add MS 21,931]

PERRERA, ISAAC, a cavalryman in St Michael's parish, Barbados, 1679. [TNA.CO1.44.47]; with 6 children {?} in St Michael's 1680. [TNA.CO1]

PERRO, DANIEL, with his wife **Hester,** and son **Daniel,** in the parish of St Magnus the Martyr, London, 1695. [LRS.1966.230]

PERRO, LIDIA, a servant, in the parish of St Katherine Coleman, London, 1695. [LRS.1966.230]

PERRYMAN, ELLINOR, a widow and a nurse, in the parish of All Hallows, Barking, London, 1695. [LRS.1966.230]

PERVERO, MOSES, an apprentice, in the parish of St Leonard, Foster Lane, London, 1695. [LRS.1966.230]

PESTANO, JOSEPH, with his wife **Hesther,** in the parish of St Katherine Cree, London, 1695. [LRS.1966.230]

PETTO, ABRAHAM, aged 21, son of **Jacob Petto,** Pearl Street, Spittalfields, Middlesex, an indentured servant bound for Virginia in 1685. [LMWB.14.181]

PHAIS, ABRAHAM, with his wife **Sarah** and child **Aron,** German Jews, were granted a pass to travel from England to Holland, 26 July 1706. [TNA.SP44.393.36]

PHARO, ISAAC, a bachelor, in the parish of St Katherine Cree, London, 1695. [LRS.1966.231]

PHILIPS, ABRAHAM, a German Jew, was granted a pass to travel from England to Holland, 30 April 1706. [TNA.SP44.390.443]

PHILIPS, BENJAMIN, a surgeon at the Middlesex Hospital, 1832. [NRS.NRAS.1500.bundle 65]

PHILIPS, GRACE AMOS, in Cincinatti, probate 1857, PCC. [TNA]

PHILIPS, JACOB, 1722. [NRS.CS271.66459]

PHILIPS, LEVI, a German Jew, was granted a pass to travel from England to Holland, 12 June 1706. [TNA.SP44.393.5]

PHILIPS, NATHAN, in Jamaica, probate 1766, PCC. [TNA]

PHILLIP, REBECHAH, aged 65, born in England, with **Harriet Phillip,** aged 25, born in England, in Howe Street, Edinburgh, 1841. [Census]

PHILIPS, SARAH, a German Jew, was granted a pass to travel from England to Holland, 30 April 1706. [TNA.SP44.390.443]

PHILLIPS, SOLOMAN, took the Oath of Abduration, at the General Quarterly Session of the Peace in Newcastle in 1733. [Newcastle Archives]

PINHEIRO, ISAAC, an alien, was granted denization 2 February 1695. [S.P.Dom.Warrant book.40.16]; resettled on Nevis, 1712. [JTP.

1709-1715.383] {son of **Abraham Pinheiro** in Amsterdam, brother of **Rachel Pinheiro** in Amsterdam and of **Sarah Mendes Goma** in Curacao}

PINHEIRO, Mrs ESTHER, merchant and ship-owner, trading between Boston and Nevis, 1716-1722, 1728-. [TNA.CO.187/1, 2]

PINTO, FERDINAND, in London, a letter, 1845. [NRS.NRAS.332.C4.844]

PINTO, JOSEPH, probate 1733 Jamaica. [BM.Add MS 21,931]

PINTE, JOSEPH, born 1759, a hairdresser from London, emigrated from London aboard the Mermaid bound for Maryland in 1774. [TNA.T47.9/11]

PINTO, ..., aged 14, a musician, from London to Aberdeen, 1800. [NRS.GD248.195.1/48]

PITMAN, NATHAN, with his wife **Hester,** in the parish of St Magnus the Martyr, London, 1695. [LRS.1966.234]

POL, JUDE, and her year old son **Moises,** were granted a pass to travel from England to Holland on 19 August 1706. [TNA.SP44.393.64]

POLAK, GETLA, a German Jew, was granted a pass to travel from England to Holland, 25 September 1706. [TNA.SP44.393.100]

POLANDER, ISAACK, with his wife **Frawcha,** in the parish of St James, Duke's Place, London, 1695. [LRS.1966.235]

POLANDER, ISRAEL, in the parish of St James, Duke's Place, London, 1695. [LRS.1966.235]

POLEMBO, MOSES, born 1754, a clerk from London, emigrated from London aboard the Britannia bound for Mahone in 1774. [TNA.T47.9/11]

POLLACK, LEVI, a merchant in Dunbar, 1776-1779. [NRS.RH15.199]

POLLETT, ISAAC, with his wife **Mary,** in the parish of St Alphage, London, 1695. [LRS.1966.235]

POOREN, ISAAC, a bachelor, in the parish of St James, Duke's Place, London, 1695. [LRS.1966.236]

PORTELLA, ISAAC, with his wife **Rachel,** and son **Abraham,** in the parish of St Katherine Cree, London, 1695. [LRS.1966.236]

PORTELLA, JACOB, in the parish of All Hallows, London Wall, 1695. [LRS.1966.236]

PORTELLA, MOSES, in the parish of All Hallows, London Wall, 1695. [LRS.1966.236]

PORTELLO, MOSES, probate 1748 Jamaica. [BM.Add MS 21,931]

POSTAN, JOSEPH, a servant, in the parish of St Gregory by St Paul's, London, 1695. [LRS.1966.237]

POTES, ELIAZER, a rope-maker, with his wife **Hannah,** and daughters **Hannah, Hester,** in the parish of St John the Baptist, London, 1695. [LRS.1966.237]

POUER, NATHAN, a German Jew, was granted a pass to travel from England to Holland, 25 September 1706. [TNA.SP44.393.99]

POUNDER, NATHAN, a book-seller, with his wife **Mary,** and daughters **Hannah, Deborah, Anne,** in the parish of St Andrew by the Wardrobe, London, 1695. [LRS.1966.237]

PRAGUE, ABRAHAM, with his wife **Rose,** and son **Herse,** in the parish of St James, Duke's Place, London, 1695. [LRS.1966.238]

PRAG, MANUEL, a servant, was granted a pass to travel from England to Holland on 6 April 1705. [TNA.SP44.390.417]

PREETT. JACOB, in St Michael's parish, Barbados, 1679. [TNA.CO1.44.47]; with 1 child{?} in St Michael's 1680. [TNA.CO1]

PRICE, JACOB, with his wife **Isabell,** in the parish of All Hallows, Barking, London, 1695. [LRS.1966.239]

PRINCE, ABRAHAM, a silk hat and fur manufacturer, at 2 Paul's Work, Edinburgh, 1822, at 14 North Bridge, and home at 4 Adam Street, Edinburgh, 1823, at 38/39 Princes Street, Edinburgh, with home at 3 Leopold Street, Edinburgh, 1825, at 49 Princes Street, Edinburgh, 1833, died 1 November 1835 aged 38. [JBGE][FJC.41]

PRINCE, ELIZA, born 1801 in Scotland, 6 Mansfield Place, Edinburgh, with **Maryann,** born 1831 in Edinburgh, 1841. [Census]

PRINCE, FANEY, born 1803 in Edinburgh, a furrier, Greenside Street, Edinburgh, with **Salinia Prince,** born 1830 in Edinburgh, **Jennet Prince,** born 1832 in Edinburgh, and **Frances Prince,** born 1834 in Edinburgh, 1841. [Census]

PRINCE, H., a fur manufacturer in Edinburgh, 1827, partner with **Abraham Prince** in A. Prince and Company, Furriers, 13 Princes Street, Edinburgh, 1828-1830. [FCJ.42]

PRINCE, HENRY, born 1806 in Ireland, a furrier, Virginia Street, Glasgow, with wife **Sophia Prince,** born 1806 in England, son **Morris Prince,** born 1833 in Glasgow, son **Elfried Prince,** born 1834 in Glasgow, daughter **Juliet Prince,** born 1836 in Glasgow, daughter **Rachel Prince,** born 1837 in Glasgow, daughter **Rosetta Prince,** born 1839 in Glasgow, and daughter **Addilade Prince,** born 1841 in Glasgow, 1841. [Census]; furrier, Argyle Arcade, Glasgow, 1829, of George Street Synagogue, 1840s. [SCJ.19/22]

PRINCE, SIMON, died 1831 aged 7. [JBGE]

PROSPENCO, DAVID, with his wife **Abigail,** son **Isaac,** and daughter **Hesther,** in the parish of St Katherine Cree, London, 1695. [LRS. 1966.240]

PROUD, GERSON, with his wife **Martha,** son **Marcom,** daughters **Elizabeth, Mary, Sarah, Hannah,** in the parish of St Michael, Crooked Lane, London, 1695. [LRS.1966.240]

PRUDA, JUDITH, a servant, in the parish of St Andrew, Undershaft, London, 1695. [LRS.1966.241]

PYKE, MYERS, in Hull, 1851. [HCA.C.DJC.4.2]

QOY, ABRAHAM, in St Michael's parish, Barbados, 1679. [TNA.CO1.44.47]; with 2 children {?} in St Michael's 1680. [TNA.CO1]

QUEEN, ISAAC, a merchant in Edinburgh, 27 November 1717. [EBR]

QUIXANO, MENDES DAVID, probate 1738 Jamaica. [BM. Add MS 21,931]

QUIXANO, MENDES ABRAHAM, probate 1738 Jamaica. [BM. Add MS 21,931]

RABGENT, ABIGAIL, a servant, in the parish of St Mary Colechurch, London, 1695. [LRS.1966.242]

RABIN, PAULUS SCIALITTI, teacher of oriental tongues at Edinburgh University ca 1665, a Jewish convert. [ERBE.1655-1685.376][OSJ.1]

RABIN, THOMAS, with his wife **Susan,** daughter **Susan,** and **John,** in the parish of Christchurch, London, 1695. [LRS.1966.242]

RAELL-DIAS, MANUELL, an alien, a grant of denization, 30 September 1668. [Patent Roll, 20 Car ii]

RAINBOW, ISAAC, apprenticed to Christ's Hospital, London, an indentured servant bound for Virginia, 1718. [Christ's Hospital Archives]

RAMES, ISAACK, with his wife **Sarah,** and **Abraham,** in the parish of St James, Duke's Place, London, 1695. [LRS.1966.242]

RAPER, MOSES, a bachelor and a silkman, in the parish of St Mary le Bow, London, 1695. [LRS.1966,243]

RAPIER, MATTHEW, with his wife **Fiduria,** sons **Matthew, Moses,** and daughter **Fiduria Stere,** in the parish of St Martin, Ironmonger Lane, London, 1695. [LRS.1966.53]

RATAM, SARAH, with sons **Isaac, Benjamin,** in the parish of All Hallows, London Wall, 1695. [LRS.1966.243]

RAYNER, AARON, 1804. [NRS.CS271.54709]

REACCA, ABRAHAM, in the parish of St Andrew Undershaft, London, 1695. [LRS.1966.245]

REISS, ISRAEL LOB, 1804. [NRS.CS271.56927]

REIS, JONAS, born 1819 or 1820 in Alsace-Lorraine, a banker and bullion merchant in Liverpool, died 25 March 1877. [Deane Road Cemetery, Liverpool]

REMONDA, JOHN, born 1744, a hairdresser from London, an indentured servant on board the Sophia bound from London to Maryland in 1774. [TNA.T47.9/11]

RENTLE, MYER M., minister of the Jew's Congregation, 19 Richmond Street, Edinburgh, father of **Moses Rintel,** 1825/1826/1827. [ED][JJC. 20]

REYSURE, ABRAHAM, on Nevis, 1678. [TNA.CO1]

REZIO, ABRAHAM LEVI, a grant of denization, 25 October 1667, [Patent Roll, 19 Car ii]; a free denizen of Barbados, 1669. [ActsPCCol.I. 531/534]

REZIO, ANTONIO RODRIGUES, a grant of denization, 11 July 1661, [Patent Roll, 13 Car ii.17]; a free denizen of Barbados, 1669. [ActsPCCol.I.531/534]

REZIO, JERONIMO RODRIGUES, an alien, residing in Barbados, a grant of denization, 20 February 1663. [Patent Roll, 15 Car ii]

RIBERO, ISAAC, probate 1745 Jamaica. [BM. Add MS 21,931]

RICARDO, ..., son of Henry David Ricardo, was born at Clifton on 23 June 1860. [GM.NS.IX.184]

RIGO, DAVID, a German Jew, was granted a pass to travel from England to Holland, 16 August 1706. [TNA.SP44/393/61]

RISSON, JUDITH, in St Michael's parish, Barbados, 1679. [TNA.CO1.44.47]; with 4 children {?} in St Michael's 1680. [TNA.CO1]

ROBLES, ANTONIO RODRIGUES, born in Fundon, Portugal, fled to Spain, Canary Islands, and England, a merchant and petitioner in London, 1656, [Cal.SPDom.cxxiv.105]; 1658. [SPDom.Commonwealth.cxxv.58]; a grant of denization, 10 June 1675. [Patent Roll, 27 Car ii part 8]

ROBBLES, JOSEPH, with his wife **Hesther,** sons **Isaac, Abraham,** and his widowed mother, in the parish of St Katherine Cree, London, 1695. [LRS.1966.250]

ROBINS, MOSES, a servant, in the parish of St Gabriel Fenchurch, London, 1695. [LRS.1966.249]

RODE, ISAAC, a German Jew, was granted a pass to travel from England to Holland, 28 February 1706. [TNA.SP44.390.390]

RODRIQUES, ABRAHAM, probate 1733 Jamaica. [BM. Add MS 21,931]

RODRIQUES, ALPHONSO, with his wife Rebecca, son Joseph, and daughter Sarah, in the parish of St Katherine Cree, London, 1695. [LRS.1966.251]

RODRIQUES, ANTHONY, in St Michael's parish, Barbados, 1679. [TNA.CO1.44.47]; with 3 children {?} in St Michael's 1680. [TNA.CO1]

RODRINGUER, DANIEL, probate 1741 Jamaica. [BM. Add MS 21,931]

RODRIQUES, or CARDOZO, DAVID, in Jamaica, probate 1815, PCC. [TNA]

RODRIQUES, GOMEZ, an alien, a grant of denization, 10 June 1675. [Patent Roll, 27 Car ii part 8]

RODRIQUES, JOHN, a bachelor, in the parish of All Hallows, London Wall, 1695. [LRS.1966.251]

RODRIGUES, JOSEPH, was granted a pass to travel from England to Holland on 6 April 1705. [TNA.SP44.390.417]

RODRIGUES, JULIAN MOSES, with his wife Rachel, sons Isaac, Aron, daughters Sarah, Hester, Judith, in the parish of All Hallows, London Wall, 1695. [LRS.1966.251]

RODRIGUES, RIBCA, was granted a pass to travel from England to Holland on 6 April 1705. [TNA.SP44.390.417]

RODRIQUES, SIMON, in the parish of St Katherine Cree, London, 1695. [LRS.1966.251]

ROLFE, ABRAHAM, a merchant, with his wife Abigail, son Samuel, daughter Abigail, and his sister Elizabeth Brandlin, in the parish of St Helen, London, 1695. [LRS.1996.252]

ROLFE, JOHN, with his wife Rebecca, son John, and daughter Sarah, in the parish of Christ Church, London, 1695. [LRS.1966.252]

ROLFE, SALATIELL, a mercer, with his wife Margaret, daughters Cybelle, Margaret, in the parish of St Katherine Cree, London, 1695. [LRS.1966.252]

ROMA, ABRAHAM, with his wife Anne, daughters Sarah, Dorothy, in the parish of Christ Church, London, 1695. [LRS.1966.252]

ROOK, JOHN HYAM, with his wife Rebecca, in the parish of St James, Duke's Place, London, 1695. [LRS.1966.253]

ROSE, REBECCA, a German Jew, was granted a pass to travel from England to Holland, 28 February 1706. [TNA.SP44.390.390]

ROSE, SARAH, a German Jew, was granted a pass to travel from England to Holland, 28 February 1706. [TNA.SP44.390.390]

ROSENBAUM, GEORGE, a pawnbroker, New Street, Gateshead, 1820. [SNE]

ROSENBAUM, HENRY, born 1816 'in foreign parts', a merchant, Gallowgate, Glasgow, with his wife Franca born 1821 'in foreign parts', son Julius born 1839 in Glasgow, and daughter Henrietta born 1840 in Glasgow. [Census]

ROSENBERG, H., and Company, manufacturing furriers and importers, 115 Union Street, Aberdeen, 1840. [Aberdeen Directory, 1840-1841]; Harris Rosenberg and his wife Alethia Barnett or Rosenberg, guilty of fireraising in Aberdeen, 1842. [CD.19]

ROSENBERG, SAMSON, born 1820, a Hebrew teacher, died 5 February 1883. [Newington MI, Edinburgh]

ROSENHEIM, BENJAMIN, born 1833, died 8 February 1895. [Piershill MI, Edinburgh]

ROSENHEIM, CHASNA, born 1835, died 12 May 1903. [Piershill MI, Edinburgh]

?? ROSS, DANIEL, [of Tompsett, Ross, & Co. in London], Hawkhill Place, Dundee, 1837; 1840. [DD]

ROSS, SIMON, with his wife **Rebecca,** in the parish of St Michael, Crooked Lane, London, 1695. [LRS.1966.253]

ROTH, RICHARD, bound from Barbados aboard the ship <u>Recovery</u> to New York, 1679. [TNA.CO1]

ROTHSCHILD, JULIAS, born 1821 in Hamburg, clerk to a linen merchant, 8 Westfield Place, Dundee, 1851. [Census]

RUBENS, MOSES ISAAC, born 1800 in Germany, a clerk, 64 St George's Road, Glasgow, wife **Jane** born 1827 in Ireland, Balmoral Place, Glasgow, died 27 November 1851, inventory 1853, Commissariat of Lanark. [NRS][Census]

RUSEL, ROSETTA, relict of **Wolfe Levy** a furrier in Glasgow, died 25 August 1857, inventory 1857, Commissariat of Lanark. [NRS]

SACERDOTE, MOSES VITTA, probate 1746 Jamaica. [BM. Add MS 21,931]

SALOM, BERNARD, an optician, 27 Hanover Street, Edinburgh, 1849, died 5 July 1859, inventory 1860, Commissariat of Edinburgh. [NRS] [EPOD]

SALOMON, ANNA, from France, permitted to sell jewels and precious stones in Edinburgh, 23 June 1669. [EBR]

SALOMONS, DAVID, born 22 November 1797 in London

SALOMON, ELIAZER, a poor Jew, was granted a pass to travel from England to Holland, 10 October 1706. [TNA.SP44.393.175]

SALOMON, GOLDA, a poor Jew, was granted a pass to travel from England to Holland, 10 October 1706. [TNA.SP44.393.178]

SALOMON, HENRY, born 17 April 1819, died 25 April 1903, husband of **Clara,** born 16 May 1819, died 28 June 1899. [Newington MI, Edinburgh]

SALOMON, HENRY EDWARD, born 1848, died 23 December 1914, husband of Marie, born 1851, died 29 April 1932. [Newington MI, Edinburgh]

SALOMON, ISAAC, a German Jew, was granted a pass to travel from England to Holland, 18 July 1706. [TNA.SP44.393.31]

SALAMONS, JACOB, took the Oath of Association in New York, 1696. [TNA]

SALOMONS, JACOBUS, took the Oath of Association in New York, 1696. [TNA]

SALOMON, LEVI, a Jew of Frankfurt, was granted a pass to travel from England to Holland and return, 16 April 1706. [TNA.SP44.390.432]

SALOMON, MARGARET, with her children, **Joachim** aged 14, and **Moses** aged 9 months, were granted a pass to travel from England to Holland on 15 August 1706. [TNA.SP44.393.59]

SALOMAN, MARCUS, a poor Jew, was granted a pass to travel from England to Holland, 10 October 1706. [TNA.SP44.393.178]

SALOMON, SAMUEL, a poor Jew, was granted a pass to travel from England to Holland, 10 October 1706. [TNA.SP44.393.178]

SALOMAN, Dr., from St Petersburg, landed in Gravesend in 1819, settled in Edinburgh by 1819. [EBR:SL115][FJC.5]

SALUMA, DAVID, with his wife **Rachel,** and daughter **Hester,** in the parish of St James, Duke's Place, London, 1695. [LRS.1966,257]

SALUMA, JACOB, a widower, in the parish of St James, Duke's Place, London, 1695. [LRS.1966.257]

SALVADOR, BRONCA, with sons **Isaac, Moses,** and daughters **Judith, Rachel,** in the parish of St Dionis, Backchurch, London, 1695. [LRS. 1966.257]

SAMSON, LYON, born 1786, an optician, Roden Place, Percy Street, Liverpool, died 1843. [Deane Road Cemetery, Liverpool]

SAMUDA, DAVID, a merchant in Lemon Street, Goodmans Fields, London, indentures, 1798, 1814. [Car.2.369; 3.25]

SAMUEL, BENJAMIN, a furrier in Bristol, 1793. [Bristol Directory, 1793/1794]

SAMUEL, DAVID, a merchant in London, attorney to **David Wolfe,** 1819. [NRS.RD5.193.713]

SAMUEL, ISAAC, a butcher in Bristol, 1793. [Bristol Directory, 1793/1794]

SAMUEL, ISRAEL, a silversmith and toyman, 22 East Street, Brighton, 1800. [Brightelmstone Directory]

SAMUEL, JACOB, a glass-engraver in Bristol, 1793. [Bristol Directory, 1793/1794]

SAMUEL, MOSES, born 1795 in London, son of **Emanuel Samuel** and his wife **Hannah Hinde,** a watchmaker and silversmith in Liverpool, died 17 April 1860, husband of **Harriet Israel,** born 1793, died 1843, parents of **Walter Samuel,** born 1820, died 1863. [Deane Road Cemetery, Liverpool]

SAMUEL, HART, born 1733, died 1806. [North Shields gravestone]

SAMUEL, LEAH, born 1842, wife of **David Goldston,** died 12 April 1916. [Newington MI, Edinburgh]

SAMUELS, PAUL STEVENS, from Jamaica, graduated MD from Edinburgh University, 1798. [EMG.29]

SAMUELS, R. S., born 1776 in Jamaica, a physician, Forres Street, Edinburgh, with **Isabella,** born 1776 in Edinburgh, 1841. [Census]

SAMUEL, RACHEL, born 1733, died 1806. [North Shields MI]

SAMUEL, SALOMON, a German Jew, was granted a pass to travel from England to Holland, 25 February 1706. [TNA.SP44.390.388]

SAMUEL, SAMUEL, aged 22, 'a cloathsman', bound from London to Friesland aboard the Princess Royal in 1774, 'for employment'. [TNA.T47.9/11]

SAMUEL, SAUEL, a decree, 23 November 1842. [NRS.SC39.17.7776]

SANDUS, DAVID, with his wife **Sarah,** sons **David, John, Joseph,** and daughter **Sarah,** in the parish of St Anne, Blackfriars, London, 1695. [LRS.1966.258]

SAQUI, ABRAHAM, born 1824 in London, a choirmaster and music teacher in Liverpool, died 1893, husband of **Julia Samuel**, born 1804, died 1865. [Deane Road Cemetery, Liverpool]

SARAH, MORDECAH, in St Michael's parish, Barbados, 1679. [TNA.CO1.44.47]; with 4 children {?} in St Michael's 1680. [TNA.CO1]

SARMENTO, JOSEPH DE CASTRO, from Portugal, graduated in medicine from Marischal College, Aberdeen, 1739. [MCA]

SAVELL, JOEL, in Jamaica, probate 1787, PCC. [TNA]

SCHACHNA, LIPMAN, a German Jew, was granted a pass to travel from England to Holland, 7 December 1705. [TNA.SP44.390.343]

SCHAN, DANIEL, probate 1735 Jamaica. [BM. Add MS 21,931]

SCHINCKINGH, BERNARD, a merchant in Barbados, a grant of denization, 15 September 1664. [Patent Roll, 16 Car ii.11]

SCHLESELMAN, GEORGE, clerk, 4 Cowgate, house 40 Perth Road, Dundee, 1853. [DD]

SCHLESELMAN, JEAN, in Broughty Ferry, 1837. [NRS.JC26.1837.140]

SCHMALZEL, JOSEPH, from Hamburg, landed in Leith, settled in Edinburgh by 1801. [FJC.5][EBR:SL115]

SCHOMBERG, RALPH, graduated MD in Aberdeen, 1745. [CJ]

SCHURICH, JOHN JACOB, probate 1731 Jamaica. [BM. Add MS 21,931]

SCHWABE, M. H., and GOBERT, merchants, 76 Brunswick Street, Glasgow, 1819, 1820. [GD][CDS][SCJ.18]

SCHWABE, RUDOLPH, born 1809 in Germany, a cotton merchant, 11 Somerset Place, Glasgow, wife **Helen**, born 1817 in Germany, daughters **Adele**, born 1840 in Germany, **Ida**, born 1845 in Germany, and **Clara**, born 1849 in Glasgow, 1851.[Census]

SCHWABE, SALIS, a member of the Merchants House of Glasgow, 1832. [SCJ.19]; letter, 1846. [NRS.GD174.1743]

SCHWABE, THEODORE A., born 1832 in Germany, a commission agent, 3 Crescent Place, Glasgow, 1851. [Census]

SCIALITTI, MOSES or PAUL, from Florence, Italy, teacher of Hebrew in Edinburgh from 1665. [OSJ.6]

SEAGROTT, GOSNELL, with his wife **Jane**, and daughter **Sarah**, in the parish of St Augustine, London, 1695. [LRS.1966.261]

SEDANCK, JACOB, a widower, with son **Abraham**, daughter **Sarah**, in the parish of St Katherine Cree, London, 1695. [LRS.1966.261]

SEEANOR, SAMUEL, 1807. [NRS.AC8.3885]

SEFFREY, PHILIP, a merchant, with his wife **Elizabeth**, in the parish of St Katherine, Coleman, London, 1695. [LRS.1966.261]

SEGNER, GEORGE, a jeweller, 'born beyond the seas', a grant of denization, 4 February 1684, [Patent Roll, 36 Car ii]; a jeweller, with his wife **Hannah**, and daughter **Sarah**, in the parish of St Mary, Woolnoth, London, 1695. [LRS.1966.261]

SELLMAN, HESTER, with her daughter **Elizabeth Gill**, in the parish of St James, Duke's Place, London, 1695. [LRS.1966,262]

SELOOVER, ISAAC, took the Oath of Association in New York, 1696. [TNA]

SEMEROWTH, GIOCAL, landed at Gravesend, from Liverpool, settled in Edinburgh by 1803, a quill-maker in Canongate. [FJC.5][EBR:SL115]

SENYOR, ISAAC, on Nevis, 1678. [TNA.CO1]

SENIOR, JACOB, from Barbados to Nevis in 1679. [TNA.C213]

SENIOR, JACOB, from Barbados aboard the bark Dove bound for Nevis 1679, [TNA.CO1]; resettled on Nevis, 1712. [JTP.1709-1715.386]

SENIOR, JOSEPH, 'born beyond the seas', residing in Barbados, a grant of denization, 27 November 1671. [Patent Roll, 23 Car ii.6]; in St Michael's parish, Barbados, 1679. [TNA.CO1.44.47]; with 3 children {?} in St Michael's 1680. [TNA.CO1]

SENIOR, JOSEPH, 1818. [NRS.AC8.6079]

SERANO, JAELL, in St Michael's parish, Barbados, 1679. [TNA.CO1.44.47]; with 1 child {?} in St Michael's 1680. [TNA.CO1]

SERENO, SOLOMON MENDEZ, 'born beyond the seas', a merchant, a grant of denization, 28 June 1682. [Patent Roll, 34 Car ii, part 2]

SERFATY, FERNANDEZ MATTAHIAS, an alien, was granted denization, 13 May 1700. [Patent Roll, 12 William III, part 4]

SERFATTY, JOSHUA, from Barbados aboard the ship Morning Star bound for Surinam in 1679. [TNA.CO1]

SERRA, ANTHONY GOMEZ, born in Penaorada, a grant of denization, 23 December 1672, [Patent Roll, 24 Car ii part 4]; a merchant in London, 1695. [ActsPCCol.II.288] [SPAWI.1695.1921]

SERRA, PHINEAS GOMEZ, 'born beyond the seas', a grant of denization, 19 March 1688. [4 Jas ii, part 6]

SERRANO, ISHAC, an alien, a merchant in Barbados, a grant of denization, 25 May 1664. [Patent Roll, 16 Car ii.3]

SERENO, SOLOMON MENDEZ, 'born beyond the seas', a merchant, a grant of denization, 28 June 1682. [Patent Roll, 34 Car ii.2]

SHACKMAN, MERIAN, a German Jew, was granted a pass to travel from England to Holland, 12 June 1706. [TNA.SP44.393.6]

SHAMMIN, HANNAH, a servant, in the parish of St Helen, London, 1695. [LRS.1966.262]

SHANK, MOSES, with his wife **Elizabeth,** son **Moses,** and daughter **Elizabeth,** in the parish of Christ Church, London, 1695. [LRS. 1966.262]

SHEAFE, ELINOUR, a widow, with daughters **Mary, Elizabeth, Elinour, Sarah, Easter,** in the parish of Christ Church, London, 1695. [LRS. 1966.262]

SHEAFE, SAMUEL, with wife **Susan,** and son **Samuel,** in the parish of All Hallows, Bread Street, London, 1695. [LRS.1966. 263]

SHEAFE, SAMUEL, a widower, in the parish of St Clement, Eastcheap, London, 1695. [LRS.1966. 263]

SHUVGIVEAN, BESTRAND, took the Oath of Association in New York, 1696. [TNA]

SILLICK, ABRAHAM, a currier and leather seller, in Side, 1820. [SNE]

SILLICK, E. & J., Pilgrim Street, Newcastle, 1820. [SNE]

SILLICK, ELIZABETH, 1812. [NRS.AC8.4632]

SILRARA, SARAH, a widow, with daughters **Rachel,** and **Rebecca,** in the parish of St Katherine Cree, London, 1695. [LRS.1966.266]

SILVA, GOMES DANIEL, probate 1743 Jamaica. [BM. Add MS 21,931]

SILVER, ABIGAIL, a widow, in the parish of St James, Duke's Place, London, 1695. [LRS.1966.266]

SILVERA, SARAH, in Jamaica, probate 1765, PCC. [TNA]

SILVERSHINE, ISRAEL COHEN, born 1805, died 1866. [Betholom MI, Birmingham]

SIMEON and LEVI, 1689. [NRS.GD18.3119]

SIMMEL, JOEL, born 1753, a hair dresser from London, an indentured servant aboard the <u>London Packet</u> bound from London to Philadelphia in 1774. [TNA.T47.9/11]

SIMMONDS, JOSEPH, born 1841, eldest son of **Samuel** and **Rebecca Simmonds** in London, died 29 March 1909, husband of **Flora,** born 1839, died 17 July 1916 eldest daughter of **Soloman** and **Leah Reach,** eldest grand-daughter of Reverend **Moses Joel.**

SIMON, HESTER BAR, in St Michael's parish, Barbados, 1679. [TNA.CO1.44.47]; with 5 children {?} in St Michael's 1680. [TNA.CO1]

SIMON, JACOB, [1], a German Jew, was granted a pass to travel from England to Holland, 17 January 1706. [TNA.SP44.390.369]

SIMON, JACOB, [2] a German Jew, was granted a pass to travel from England to Holland, 22 January 1706. [TNA.SP44.390.369]

SIMONS, MICHAEL, settled in Glasgow 1849, a fruit broker and politician, Deputy Lieutenant of the County of the City of Glasgow in 1905. [ASJ.5]

SIMONS, Reverend S., in Hull, 1852. [HCA.C.DJC.2.1.12.4]

SINGER, ISAAC, in Jamaica, probate 1802, PCC. [TNA]

SKLOVSKY, SALOMON, born 1849, died 2 February 1934. [Newington MI, Edinburgh]

SMARGIN, ABRAHAM, a planter, resettled on Nevis 1712. [JTP. 1712.386]

SOLOMANS, ABRAHAM, in Rhode Island, part owner of the ship Confirmation, 1769. [ActsPCCol.V.192]

SOLOMON, CHARLES, watchmaker, 95 Nicolson Street, Edinburgh, 18.... [FJC.42]

SOLOMON, DAVID, charged with a breach of the peace in Hackney, London, 18 December 1738. [JH.283]

SOLOMON, EVE, in the parish of St Andrew, Undershaft , London, 1695. [LRS.1966.274]

SOLOMON, GODFREY, born 1771, died 21 November 1857. [Betholom MI, Birmingham]

SOLOMON, ISAAC, an embroiderer and an affiliate of Lodge St David in Edinburgh in 1761. [OJS.10]

SOLOMON, ISRAEL, from Poland, a dealer in Hull, 1797. [HCA.C.BRE. 7.1.54]

SOLOMON, JOSEPH, aged 19, 'a cloathsman', bound from London to Friesland aboard the Princess Royal in 1774, 'for employment'. [TNA.T47.9/11]

SOLOMON, JULIUS, born 1826 'in foreign parts', Cambridge Street, Glasgow, 1841. [Census]

SOLOMON, MARIA, daughter of **Dr Solomon**, Gillead House, Liverpool, married **Moses Lemon** a surgeon on 1 February 1815. [SM.77.236]

SOLOMON, Mrs MARY, relict of **Napthali Hart** a watchmaker in London, died in Edinburgh on 22 June 1853, inventory 1853, Commissariat of Edinburgh. [NRS]

SOLOMON, MATILDA, born 1778 'in foreign parts', 7 Hill Place, Edinburgh, 1841. [Census]

SOLOMON, MATILDA, died 23 March 5608 aged 19. [JBGE]

SOLOMON, MOSES, a dealer in silk, Edinburgh, 1823, at 17 Carnegie Street, Edinburgh, 1832. [FJC.42]

SOLOMON, MOSES, born 1801 in foreign parts', West Nicholson Street, Edinburgh, 1841. [Census]

SOLOMONS, MOSES, in Edinburgh, 1849. [NRS.AD14.49.164]

SOLOMON, PHILIP, a furrier and capmaker, North Richmond Street, Edinburgh, 1827, father of **Alexander Philips**. [FJC.18/42]

SOLOMON, S., a jeweller, 165 Rose Street, Edinburgh, 1819. [FJC.42]

SOLOMON, S., in St Helena, an account, 1832. [NRS.GD45.5.88]

SOLOMAN, SAMUEL, graduated MD in Aberdeen, 1796. [CJ]

SOLOMON, Dr SAMUEL, of Gilead House, Liverpool, died in Bath in 1819. [SM.83.587]

SOLOMON, SIMON, in the parish of St Andrew, Undershaft, London, 1695. [LRS.1966.274]

SOLOMONS, SOLOMON, charged with a breach of the peace in Hackney, London, 18 December 1738. [JH.283]

SOLOMAN, ..., a musician, from London to Aberdeen, 1800. [NRS.GD248.195.1/48]

SOLOMON, Mrs, aged 38, wife of **Dr Solomon** of Gilead House, Liverpool, died there in 1819. [SM.93.587]

SOLOMONS, versus ISRAEL, an appeal from Jamaica, 1774. [ActsPCCol.unbound papers #928]

SORRACO, MOSES, with his wife **Hesther,** and daughter **Rebecca,** in the parish of St Katherine Cree, London, 1695. [LRS.1966.274]

SOUSA, ABRAHAM, in St Michael's parish, Barbados, 1679. [TNA.CO1.44.47]; with 3 children {?} in St Michael's 1680. [TNA.CO1]

SOUZA, LOUIS RODRIGUES, ship-owner in Amsterdam, 1709. [NRS.AC10.86]

SOUZA, SIMEON RODRIGUES, ship-owner in Amsterdam, 1709. [NRS.AC10.86]

SPENCER, BENJAMIN, translator on the Scots Expedition to Darien on the Isthmus of Panama, 1698, captured by the Spanish and imprisoned in Seville on a charge of piracy; landed at Matanzas, Cuba, deposition 25 September 1699. [NRS.GD406.1.4541][Audienca de Panama, General Archives of the Indies, Seville, #160/1 {2540}{69-6-6}][JPD]

SPINOZA, MOSES, an alien, was granted denization, 4 November 1699. [Patent Roll, 11 William III, pt.3.]

SPRANGER, ABRAHAM, in the parish of St Martin, Vintry, London, 1695. [LRS.1966.276]

SPRINGER, BENJAMIN, formerly of St Augustine, Florida, lately of St Luke, London, probate 1786, PCC. [TNA]

STANKIE, GEORGE & HENRY, cap manufacturers in Edinburgh, 1850. [NRS.CS280.12.58]

STANKIE, GERSON, born 1807 'in foreign parts', a farrier, 7 Hill Place, Edinburgh, with **Hannah,** born 1813 'in foreign parts', and **Henry Stankie,** born 1829 'in foreign parts', 1841. [Census]

STENBURGH, SOLOMON, shochet in Glasgow, 1826. [SCJ.19]

STERRIKER, HANNAH, born 1762, a servant, emigrated from Hull aboard the Two Friends to Nova Scotia in 1774. [TNA.T47.9/11]

STEVENS, ..., servant of General Wessely, 1721. [NAS.GD158.1951]

STOCKEMAN, ISAAC, born in Hamburg, son of **Isaac Stockeman,** a grant of naturalization, 1670. [Patent Roll, 22 Car ii.137]

STOLLER, ANNE, wife of **Tobias Stoller,** born 1849, died 17 January 1913, [Piershill MI, Edinburgh]

STRAUSE, ELIAS, bound from Barbados aboard the ship Experiment for London in 1679. [TNA.CO1]

STROLOGER, Miss, a linen draper, Sandhill, Newcastle, 1790. [Newcastle Directory]

STUNGO, ELIAS, born 1819, died 26 January 1903. [Newington MI, Edinburgh]

STUNGO, MOSES, born 1848, died 30 December 1932. [Newington MI, Edinburgh]

SUAREZ, ABRAHAM, a Jew in Barbados, 1665. [SPAWI.1665.949]

SUAREZ, BENJAMIN, in the parish of St James, Duke's Place, London, 1695. [LRS.1966.283]

SUARIS, DAVID, in St Michael's parish, Barbados, 1679. [TNA.CO1.44.47]

SUECUS, SAMUEL, matriculated at Marischal College, Aberdeen, in 1634. [MCA]

SUIERO, or SUCIRO, ABRAHAM, an alien, was granted denization 2 February 1695. [S.P.Dom.Warrant book.40.16]

SURA, JUDA, a German Jew, was granted a pass to travel from England to Holland, 25 September 1706. [TNA.SP44.393.100]

SWAILE, SOLOMON, with his wife **Lydia,** in the parish of All Hallows, Barking, London, 1695. [LRS.1966.284]

SWARIS, DAVID, with 5 children {?} in St Michael's 1680. [TNA.CO1]

SWEARAS, ABRAHAM, with his wife **Sarah,** in the parish of St Gabriel, Fenchurch, London, 1695. [LRS.1966.285]

SWEAVIS, ABRAHAM HENERICUS, with his wife **Sarah,** sons **Jacob, Isaac, Samuel,** daughters **Brunea, Esther,** in the parish of St Katherine Cree, London, 1695. [LRS.1966.285]

SYMONS, GEORGE, born 1772, from Amsterdam, settled in Leith by 1798, shopman in service of **Lion Davis,** by 1810 he was an umbrella maker in the Luckenbooths of Edinburgh, in 1815 he was at 184 High Street, Edinburgh; an umbrella maker, Easter Road, Edinburgh, 1841, with wife **Helen,** born Edinburgh, 1781, daughter **Sarah,** born 1824 South Leith, daughter **Margaret,** born South Leith 1827, **Alexander** born 1829 South Leith, and daughter **Jessie,** born 1831 in South Leith. [FJC.5/42][EBR:SL115][Census]

SYMON, ISAAC, 1761. [NRS.CS271.13224]

SYMONS, SAMUEL, from Barbados bound for New York in 1678. [TNA.CO1]

SYMONDS, SAMUEL, a militiaman in Barbados, 1679. [TNA.CO1.44.47]

TABER, GIDEON, in Rhode Island, probate 1765, PCC. [TNA]

TALLIS, ARON, with his wife **Judith,** sons **Benjamin, George,** and daughter **Rebecca,** in the parish of All Hallows, London Wall, 1695. [LRS.1966.285]

TALLIS, ISAAC, a widower, with his sons **Moses, Joseph,** and daughters **Sarah, Rachel,** in the parish of St Katherine Cree, London, 1695. [LRS. 1966.285]

TALLIS, MARY, in the parish of All Hallows, London Wall, 1695. [LRS. 1966.285]

TAPLAN, ISAAC, aged 16, a laborer from Somerset, emigrated from London aboard the <u>Adventure</u> bound for Maryland in 1775. [TNA.T47.9/11]

TARTES, ABRAHAM, a poor Jew, was granted a pass to travel from England to Holland, 10 October 1706. [TNA.SP44.393.172]

TAVARES, ABRAHAM, the younger, late of Jamaica, dead by 1798, an indenture. [Car.3.25]

TAVAREZ, DAVID, probate 1746 Jamaica. [BM. Add MS 21,931]

TAXERA, JACOB, with his wife **Sarah,** in the parish of St Katherine Cree,   London, 1695. [LRS.1966.286]

TEIXERA, SARAH, was granted a pass to travel from England to Holland on 6 April 1705. [TNA.SP44.390.417]

TEDMAN, BENJAMIN, with his wife **Mary,** and daughter **Pagge,** in the parish of   St Dunstan in the East, London, 1695. [LRS.1966.288]

TEMPLO, JACOB JEHUDA LEON, a heraldic draughtsman, visited England in 1675. [TJS.ii.156]

TENOCK, ABRAM, a militiaman in Barbados, 1679. [TNA.CO1.44.47]

TENOCK, JACOB, a militiaman in Barbados, 1679. [TNA.CO1.44.47]

TERDOTT, ABRAHAM, with his wife **Rose,** sons **Solomon, David, Zephra,** in the parish of St James, Duke's Place, London, 1695. [LRS. 1966.288]

TIMIUS, MYERS, a seal wax maker from Breslau, Prussia, settled in Edinburgh by 1793. [EBR.SL115]

TINICO, JACOB, from Barbados aboard the ketch William and John bound for to New England in 1679. [TNA.CO1]

TIPNIWASOW, DAVID, a bachelor and a merchant, in the parish of St Margaret Lothbury, London, 1695. [LRS.1966.292]

TISSO, JOHN, with his wife **Susan,** and son **David,** in the parish of St Anne, Aldersgate, London, 1695. [LRS.1966.292]

TONCKY, NEHEMIAH, in the parish of St Michael, Crooked Lane, London, 1695. [LRS.1966.293]

TORRES, DAVID LOPES, a merchant in Jamaica, executor of Isaac Lamego, 1775, [Car.3.155]; probate 1816 PCC. [TNA]

TORRES, ISAAC LOPES, an executor, 1802. [Car.2.367]

TORRES, SARAH LOPES, a widow by 1775, [Car.3.155]; probate 1787 PCC. [TNA]

TOREZ, JUDIEAH, in St Michael's parish, Barbados, 1679. [TNA.CO1.44.47]; with 2 children {?} in St Michael's 1680. [TNA.CO1]

TOREZ, LOPEZ SARAH, probate 1735 Jamaica. [BM. Add MS 21,931]

TREIBER, DANIEL, a bachelor and a servant, in the parish of St Helen, London,   1695. [LRS.1966.295]

TRYTLE, JOEL, a jeweller, Tyne Street, North Shields, 1824. [Newcastle Directory]

TUNCKS, SARAH, with her son **Symon,** and daughter **Sarah,** in the parish of St Faith under St Paul's, London, 1695. [LRS.1966.206]

TUNIMAN, SIMON, a bachelor and a merchant, in the parish of St Mary le Bow, London, 1695. [LRS.1966.297]

USHER, HEZECHIAH, a merchant in London, 1675. [TNA.E190.62.1]

VAGOR, ESTHER, in the parish of St Katherine Cree, London, 1695. [LRS.1966.299]

VALE, JACOB FONCECO, in St Michael's parish, Barbados, 1679. [TNA.CO1.44.47]; with 5 children{?} in St Michael's 1680. [TNA.CO1]

VALENTIA, ISAAC, with his wife **Rachel,** in the parish of St Katherine Cree,   London, 1695. [LRS.1966.300]

VALLERY, ABRAHAM, died in Edinburgh, 1831. [JBGE]

VALUERDE, ABRAHAM, in St Michael's parish, Barbados, 1679. [TNA.CO1.44.47]; with 2 children {?} in St Michael's 1680. [TNA.CO1]

VANE, BENJAMIN, a German Jew, was granted a pass to travel from England to Holland, 3 January 1706. [TNA.SP44.390.362]

VAN OVEN, Dr JOSHUA, born 1766, a surgeon and educationalist in London and Liverpool, died 3 February 1838. [Deane Road Cemetery, Liverpool]

VEGA, GULIELMO, an alien, a grant of denization, 10 June 1675. [Patent Roll. 27 Car ii.8]

VENIAD, MINELEER, in the parish of St Katherine Cree, London, 1695. [LRS.1966.301]

VERBRUGH, SALOMON, was granted a pass to travel from England to Holland, 22 June 1706. [TNA.SP44.393.13]

VERDUGO, AARON, probate 1745 Jamaica. [BM. Add MS 21,931]

VERES, RACHEL, a widow, with her son **Samson,** his wife **Joyce,** their daughters **Hester, Grace,** in the parish of St Andrew Undershaft, London, 1695. [LRS.1966.301]

VEYARDOE, DEBORAH, in the parish of St Michael, Bassishaw, London, 1695. [LRS.1966.301]

VIELL, LODOVICUS, a Jewish convert in Edinburgh, 1687. [ERBE. 1681-1680.205]

VIERA, JOSEPH, a merchant in Amsterdam, 1712. [NRS.AC8.152]

VOICE, GAMALIEL, a bachelor, in the parish of St Margaret, Lothbury, London, 1695. [LRS.1966.301]

WAAG, MOSES, probate 1745 Jamaica. [BM. Add MS 21,931]

WAGAR, JOHN, with his wife **Tabitha,** in the parish of St Mary Somerset, London, 1695. [LRS.1966.302]

WAINHOUSE, JOHN, a painter, with his wife **Hester,** son **John,** daughter **Hester,** in the parish of St Matthew Bassishaw, London, 1695. [LRS.1966.302]

WALBERRY, JOHN, with his wife **Alice,** daughter **Rebecca,** in the parish of All Hallows, London Wall, 1695. [LRS.1966.302]

WALDENFIELD, SAMUEL, with his wife **Mary,** in the parish of St Dionis Backchurch, London, 1695. [LRS.1966.303]

WALDMAN, ABRAHAM, from Hamburg, was granted a pass to travel from England to Holland, 15 March 1706. [TNA.SP44.390.397]

WALDRON, JUDAH, with son **John,** daughters **Elizabeth, Mary,** in the parish of St Augustine, London, 1695. [LRS.1966.303]

WALKER, ABRAHAM, with his wife **Hannah,** son **Abraham,** daughter **Hannah,** in the parish of St Helen, London, 1695. [LRS.1966.303]

WALKER, GEORGE, with his wife **Damaras,** and daughter **Damaras,** in the parish of St Lawrence Jewry, London, 1695. [LRS.1966.303]

WALKER, JOSEPH, with his wife **Judith,** and daughter **Judith,** in the parish of St Michael le Querne, London, 1695. [LRS.1966.303]

WALLEE, JONATHAN, with his wife **Sarah,** in the parish of St Margaret Pattens, London, 1695. [LRS.1966.304]

WALLWIN, ABRAHAM, with his son **Abraham,** in the parish of St Mary Abchurch, London, 1695. [LRS.1966.304]

WALLRAND, MOSES, a servant, in the parish of St Anne, Blackfriars, London, 1695. [LRS.1966.305]

WALLRAND, ROBERT, with daughters **Rebecca, Sarah,** and sons **Shunamite, Robert,** in the parish of St Anne, Blackfriars, London, 1695. [LRS.1966.305]

WARD, BENJAMIN, with his wife **Abigail,** daughter **Abigail,** son **James,** n the parish of St Margaret, New Fish Street London, 1695. [LRS. 1966.305]

WARD, MOSES, a man servant, in the parish of St Ethelburga, London, 1695. [LRS.1966.306]

WASH, SAMUEL, a German Jew, was granted a pass to travel from England to Holland, 15 January 1706. [TNA.SP44.390.368]

WASSERZUG, MICHAEL, born 1837, died 7 June 1898. [Newington MI, Edinburgh]

WEBLING, MOSES, an apprentice, in the parish of St Michael le Querne, London, 1695. [LRS.1966.310]

WEINBERG, Mrs AGNES, born 4 June 1846, wife of **Isaac Julius Weinberg,** died 26 November 1936. [Balgay MI, Dundee]

WEINBERG, ISAAC, born 1832 in Hamburg, a merchant's clerk, 111 Nethergate, Dundee, 1851, [Census], a Justice of the Peace, died 1 January 1912. [Balgay MI, Dundee]

WEHRLE, D., clock and watch maker, 106 Murraygate, Dundee, 1853. [DD]

WELLDELL, JOHN, with his wife **Hannah,** daughter **Hannah,** in the parish of St Mildred, Poultry, London, 1695. [LRS.1966.311]

WESSELS, ABRAHAM, a merchant in London, 1667. [Cal.SPDom.ccix. 135]

WETH, HACHBETH, on Nevis, 1708. [TNA.CO.152-157]

WINSER, SOLLOME, in the parish of Christchurch, London, 1695. [LRS. 1966.323]

WITENAR, MATHEW, a German Jew, was granted a pass to travel from England to Holland, 17 December 1705. [TNA.SP44.390.347]

WOLFE, DAVID, a merchant in Kingston, Jamaica, a deed, 1819. [NRS.RD5.193.713]

WOLFE, ELLIS, merchant in Kingston, Jamaica, 1819, late in Killingdon, Middlesex, England, deceased, reference in **David Wolfe's** deed. [NRS.RD5.193.713]

WOLFE, EMANUELL, aboard the Thomas and Susan bound for Boston in 1679. [TNA.CO1]

WOLF, FREDRICK, born 1811 'in foreign parts', a hawker, St Mary Wynd, Edinburgh, 1841. [Census]

WOLF, H. F., born 1796 'in foreign parts', a teacher, 148 High Street, Glasgow, with **Henry F. Wolf,** born 1835 'in foreign parts', 1841. [Census]

WOLFE, JOHN REISSBERG, graduated MD from Glasgow University, 1856. [RGG.657]

WOLFE, MARGARET, 1819, reference in **David Wolfe's** deed. [NRS.RD5.193.713]

WOOLF, HENRY, born in Prussia, grant of naturalisation, 4 March 1845. [TNA.HO1.18.79]

WOOLFF, MAXIMILIAN, in Manchester, Jamaica, married **Maria Cohen,** daughter of **Hyman Cohen** in London on 19 September 1821. [GM. 91.372]

WOLFF, MAXIMILIAN JOSEPH, aged 67, died in Norfolk Square, Hyde Park, London, on 12 May 1856. [GM.NS.XLV.667]

WOLFENDEN, ANNA, an alien, a grant of denization, in June 1670. [Patent Roll, 22 Car ii]

WOOLFENDEN, HESTER, a servant, in the parish of St Helen, London, 1695. [LRS.1966.327]

WOOLFENDEN, JEREMIAH, from Barbados to Nevis in 1679. [TNA.CO1]

???WOODRUFFE, JOSEPH, took the Association Oath in Barbados, 1696. [TNA]

XIMENES, DANIEL, late of Gower Street, now of Duke Street, Portland Place, London, administrator of his deceased wife **Sarah,** an indenture, 1802. [Car.2.367]

YANIAVIECZ, FELIX, a settlement deed, 5 March 1848. [NAS.RD5.815.550]

YDANA, ISAAC, probate 1733 Jamaica. [BM. Add MS 21,931]

YDANA, JOSEPH, probate 1748 Jamaica. [BM. Add MS 21,931]

YDANA, MOSES, probate 1741 Jamaica. [BM. Add MS 21,931]

YOFFE, JOSEPH, born 1847, died 14 October 1911. [Piershill MI, Edinburgh]

YOWELL, JOSEPH, with his wife **Judith,** sons **Abraham, Pere,** in the parish of St James, Duke's Place, London. 1695. [LRS.1966.331]

ZACKASH, SAMUEL, an Admiralty Court decreet, 1819. [NRS.AC8.6494]

ZEIGLER, ALEXANDER, a jeweller, 7 Nicolson Square, Edinburgh, 1815. [FJC.43]

ZEIGLER, ALEXANDER, a surgeon, at 4 Patrick Square, Edinburgh, 1820, at 37 Nicolson Street, Edinburgh, 1824, and at 17 Carnegie Street, Edinburgh, 1833; medical student in Edinburgh, 1813-1816, LRCSE 1816, FRCPE 1853, graduated MD 6 May 1845 at St Andrews; a surgeon in Edinburgh, died 10 April 1863. [FJC.43][BRUA.979]

ZEIGLER, JO., a jeweller, 17 Niddry Street, Edinburgh, house at 37 Nicolson Street, Edinburgh, 1815. [FJC.43]

ZEIGLER, WILLIAM, from Scotland, graduated MD from Edinburgh University in 1850. [EMG.146]

ZELDA, FEIGE, born 1829, died 21 December 1910. [Piershill MI, Edinburgh]

ZEMPLEBURGH, S. S., a watchmaker and jeweller, at 3 Eldin Street, Edinburgh, later a teacher of German, Hebrew, and Chaldee, 6 Roxburgh Place, Edinburgh, 1835. [EPOD][FJC.17/43]

ZENI, SALOMON, a poor Jew, was granted a pass to travel from England to Holland, 10 October 1706. [TNA.SP44/393/178]

ZILBERMAN, JANETTA, born 1834, widow of **Michael Wasserzug,** died 22 December 1903, parents of **Maurice Wasserzug** in Johannesburg. [Newington MI, Edinburgh]

..............., **SIMCA,** with her daughter **Simca,** German Jews, were granted a pass to travel from England to Holland, 25 September 1706. [TNA.SP44/393/100]

REFERENCES

ActsPCCol. =   Acts of the Privy Council, Colonial, series, London

AD   =   Aberdeen Directory

BM   =   British Museum

BRO   =   Bristol Record Office

BRUA   =   Biographical Register of the University of

                St Andrews, 1747-1897, [St Andrews, 2004]

Car	=	Caribbeana, series, [London, 1909-1919]
CDS	=	Commercial Directory of Scotland & N. England
CJ	=	Caledonian Jews, [London, 2009]
CLRO	=	City of London Record Office
CTP	=	Calendar of Treasury Papers, series, [London, 1871]
DD	=	Dundee Directory
EBR	=	Edinburgh Burgh Records/Burgess Roll
ELD	=	Edinburgh and Leith Directory, [Edinburgh, 1859]
EMG	=	Graduates in Medicine, University of Edinburgh, from 1705 to 1856, [Edinburgh, 1867]
EPOD	=	Edinburgh Post Office Directory, [Edinburgh, 1835]
ERBE	=	Extracts from the Records of the Burgh of Edinburgh
FJC in	=	A History of the Origins of the First Jewish Community Scotland, Abel Phillips, [Edinburgh, 1979]
GBR	=	Glasgow Burgess Roll
GM	=	Gentleman's Magazine, series
HCA	=	Hull City Archives
JBGE	=	Jewish Burial Ground, Edinburgh
JPD	=	The Darien Disaster, [London, 1968]
JH	=	Justice in 18th Century Hackney, [London, 1991]
JTP	=	Journal of the Commissioners for Trade and the Plantations, series
KCA	=	Officers and Graduates of University and King's College, Aberdeen, 1495-1860, [Aberdeen, 1893]
LMD	=	Lord Mayor of London Depositions

LRS	=	London Record Society
MCA	=	Records of Marischal College and Aberdeen University, [Aberdeen,1889]
MI	=	Monumental Inscription
NAS	=	National Archives of Scotland, Edinburgh
NRS	=	National Records of Scotland, Edinburgh
OSJ	=	The Origins of Scottish Jewry by A. Levy, in Transactions of the Jewish Historical Society of England Vol. xix
OU	=	Oxford University
RGG	=	Roll of Graduates of the University of Glasgow, [Glasgow, 1898]
SCHR	=	Scottish Church History Records, series, Edinburgh
SCJ	=	Second City Jewry. K.E. Collins, [Glasgow, 1990]
SM	=	Scots Magazine, series, Edinburgh
SNE	=	Commercial Directory of Scotland and Northern England,[Manchester, 1820]
SP	=	State Papers
SPAWI	=	Calendar of State Papers, America and the West Indies, Series, London
TJS	=	Transactions of the Jewish Historical Society of England
TNA	=	The National Archives, London

www.ingramcontent.com/pod-product-compliance
Lightning Source LLC
Chambersburg PA
CBHW070926270326
41927CB00011B/2741